DESERT

The Earth series traces the historical significance and cultural history of natural phenomena. Written by experts who are passionate about their subject, titles in the series bring together science, art, literature, mythology, religion and popular culture, exploring and explaining the planet we inhabit in new and exciting ways.

Series editor: Daniel Allen

Desert

Roslynn D. Haynes

REAKTION BOOKS

For my husband Raymond and our daughters Nicola and Rowena, who have shared my fascination with deserts

Published by
Reaktion Books Ltd
33 Great Sutton Street
London EC1V 0DX, UK
www.reaktionbooks.co.uk

First published 2013

Printed and bound in China by Toppan Printing Co. Ltd.

A catalogue record for this book is available from the British Library

ISBN 978 1 78023 169 3

CONTENTS

Preface

The grandeur of deserts derives from their being, in their aridity,
the negative of the earth's surface and of our civilized humours.
They are places where humours and fluids become rarefied, where
the air is so pure that the influence of the stars descends direct from
the constellations . . . a silence that exists nowhere else.
Jean Baudrillard, *America* (1986)

'Desert' is not an innocent term. Geographically it is defined in
terms of rainfall, but unlike other landforms there is, inbuilt in
its very name, a sense of foreboding. The English word 'desert'
and its equivalents in the Romance languages all derive from
the Latin *desertum*, meaning 'abandoned', which is also the sense
of the Egyptian *tesert*. In Hindi the original meaning of the
word for desert, *marustahal*, was 'a place of death', and the name
of the Taklamakan Desert is most likely the Uyghur version of
an Arabic word meaning 'a place to leave alone'. Given the strong
probability in deserts of dying from heat, cold, starvation or
thirst, or of becoming disoriented and lost, these connotations
are unsurprising.

Deserts also threaten the inner self. Their immensity, solitude
and silence pose questions about identity and meaning that are
not easily dismissed. As the British explorer Ernest Giles (1835–
1897) wrote of his experience in the Australian desert:

> I felt somewhat lonely and cogitated that what has been
> written or said by cynics, solitaries, or Byrons of the delights
> of loneliness, has no real home in the human heart. Nothing
> could appal the mind so much as the contemplation of
> eternal solitude.[1]

Yet for many people deserts have been intensely alluring. For
the Old Testament prophets and the Desert Fathers they were
places of purification and spiritual renewal; explorers have sought

Sossusvlei salt pan,
Namib Desert, 2009.

out deserts 'for the burning charm of seeking something new' and to be the first to set foot there;[2] for travellers, the attraction is often the challenge of life at the edge, braving extremes of heat, cold and endurance, or discovering a place to regain simplicity and a sense of priorities; for artists, deserts mean brilliant colours, simplified forms and clarity of vision; for astronomers, they provide the dry atmosphere that grants them the best observing conditions from Earth; for writers, they represent silence, solitude, the edge of the sacred; for many indigenous peoples, desert is home.

This book explores the great diversity of the world's deserts, hot, cold, coastal, inland, sandy, rocky and salt, and includes the largest desert of all: ice-bound Antarctica. We know now that on a geological time scale, deserts are transitory: they have appeared and disappeared, leaving a trail of intriguing evidence, from marine fossils to cave paintings, that tells us about their former state. Even more diverse than deserts themselves are the astonishing adaptations of plants and animals to these life-threatening environments, and the human societies that have managed to survive here, leaving records of their life in art and in millennia-old mummies, but almost everywhere experiencing new hardships in their economic and political struggles. Equally intriguing is the question of why the world's great monotheistic religions all arose in the desert and what influence, if any, the ethical values ascribed to it continue to have on believers. The next three chapters engage with those who have constructed the deserts of our imagination: explorers and travellers who recorded their fascinating stories and the motives that lured them into strange and dangerous places; the writers and film-makers who envisaged and peopled these alien landscapes; and the artists and photographers who have persuaded us to look past monotony to new and beautiful aspects of deserts.

The cultural geographer Yi-Fu Tuan has pointed out that, from the time of Herodotus, the most common Western response to deserts has been denial of their existence, resulting from either ignorance, a desire to preserve the reputation of the Creator from the slur of bringing such appalling places into existence,[3] or – in

Erg Chebbi, Morocco, 2005.

the case of North America and Australia – a wilful and irrational optimism about the anticipated bounty of the new land. Now the danger is more often that we will deny our responsibility for preserving these once pristine but now endangered places.

1 The Diversity of Deserts

A desert is a place without expectation.

Nadine Gordimer, 'Pula' (1973)

Typically we envisage deserts as vast, permanent expanses of hot sand, with perhaps a distant oasis indicated by a palm tree in silhouette. But in fact the world's deserts vary greatly in age, landforms, stability, surface features, temperature, flora, fauna and culture so that our stereotypes apply to very few desert regions. We might not even include Antarctica, the world's largest desert, in our mental picture. To avoid ambiguity, deserts are now defined as areas with an average of less than 250 mm (10 in) of precipitation a year, or where evapotranspiration exceeds precipitation; but even within this range deserts vary greatly. In some parts of the Atacama in western South America no rain has been recorded in 400 years, whereas in Australia, desert areas where for decades there were only dry watercourses may be inundated in one season by flooding rivers. After rain, deserts typically become gardens, bursting into flower and attracting insects and the reptiles and birds that feed on them.

Contrary to the stereotype, only one-fifth of the world's deserts are covered with sand. These are the great ergs, areas of shifting, undulating dunes resembling ocean waves. But there are four other main desert landforms: mountain and basin deserts; hard, rocky plateaus or *hamada*, formed when wind removes the fine sand particles; stony plains or regs, which may appear as cobbled pavements; and inter-montane basins characterized by salt flats.

Deserts are as varied in age as they are in appearance. On a geological time scale they appear and disappear. We know from

rock art in the area that 12,000 years ago, at the end of the last ice age, the Sahara and the now arid, mountainous Gilf Kebir ('Great Barrier') in southwestern Egypt were well-watered, wooded savannah, supporting water-dependent animals such as crocodiles, hippopotamuses, elephants, cattle and antelope, and that they remained so as recently as 2,000 years ago. Fossils of dinosaurs have been found in Algeria, indicating a time of lush vegetation. Earlier still, 150–200 million years ago (MYA), the Sahara was submerged beneath an ancient sea up to 5,000 m deep, whose creatures remain as fossils beneath the sand; 800 m underground there is still a vast reservoir of fossil water, sealed in an aquifer of impervious rock for thousands of years and remaining clean and fresh. Antarctica once sustained dense forests, while some 100 MYA, in the Cretaceous Period, the Central Australian desert was a vast inland sea, the Eromanga Sea, home to whale-sized marine reptiles, pliosaurs and plesiosaurs, ichthyosaurs and squid-like belemnites.

Deserts may also disappear. Geologists believe that some five and a half MYA the entire area of the Mediterranean Sea was a

Sand dunes in Tadrart Acacus mountain range, western Libya, part of the Sahara.

low-lying desert separated from the Atlantic Ocean by a land bridge joining Africa and Europe. When the Ice Age ended and the sea levels rose, the Atlantic poured in, gradually filling this immense desert basin.[1]

In terms of temperature there are hot or subtropical deserts, cold winter deserts, cool coastal deserts and icy polar deserts, while inland deserts like the Sahara, the Arabian and the Asian deserts, with no cloud cover as insulation, typically experience great diurnal changes in temperature, from baking heat of up to 58°c around noon to below freezing at night.

Hot Deserts

The best known of the hot deserts is the Sahara (the word means 'desert' in Arabic), the world's largest desert after Antarctica. Stretching 4,800 km across North Africa through thirteen countries, it is home to some 4 million people.[2] Although it has provided the prototype for Western ideas of 'desert', the Sahara includes a wide range of landforms and surfaces: mountains, stone pavements, gravel, vast areas of wind-blown sand dunes, ergs and volcanic mountains such as the 900-m Hoggar Massif. In the Ennedi Range of Chad, in the Tadrart Acacus region of Libya and in southern Algeria, wind and sand erosion have sculpted hundreds of natural arches, while the Tassili n'Ajjer Massif in the central Sahara is a strange lunar landscape of steep gorges and spectacular rock formations. In ancient times rivers gushed down this massif, whose name in Berber means 'plateau of the rivers', carving deep valleys and filling huge lakes that today are the great ergs, while in more recent dry periods wind erosion has created rock formations that resemble stone forests.

Long before Lawrence of Arabia captivated the West with romantic images of desert Bedouin, the Arabian Desert and its traditional inhabitants held a fascination for the Western mind, woven from stories of the Crusades, nineteenth-century travellers' tales of danger and disguise, and associations with harems and the holy places of Islam forbidden to infidels. Visually the Arabian Desert is a panorama of vivid colours – yellow sand and coloured

rocks outlined against a brilliant blue sky – but most travellers
retain an overwhelming impression of vast, empty space and total
silence, except when sand storms roar through the landscape,
obliterating every feature and burying a tent in minutes.

Geographically the Arabian Peninsula is an immense plateau
sloping from the steep Asir and Hejaz Mountains on the western
side and ending in escarpments on the other three sides. Stretching
from Yemen to the Persian Gulf, it includes three large sand
desert areas: the Syrian or Hamad Desert; the An Nafud in the

Arch of Fozzigiaren in
Tadrart Acacus, Libya,
2007.

Tassili n'Ajjer National
Park, Algeria, 2009.

The Rub' al Khali, or Empty Quarter, is the largest sand desert on earth, 2008.

north, a sea of enormous shifting sand dunes; and the hyper-arid Rub' al Khali, the notorious 'Empty Quarter' of southern Arabia, with an annual rainfall of only 35 mm. Its sand, heaped into dunes up to 250 m high, is formed mostly of silicates, coated with iron oxide that colours it red, purple and orange. The Arabian Desert also includes limestone cliffs, plateaux and canyons in the Jebel Tuwaiq region, and the treacherous quicksands of Umm al Samim, while in the west are eighteen volcanic areas, mainly in Hejaz. Yemen in the south was called 'Arabia Felix' by the Romans because of its relatively high rainfall and easy access by sea, making it the main source of frankincense and myrrh and a trading post for spices from the East. In the far east, in Oman, lie the Wahiba Sands, an area of dunes and wadis now occupied solely by Bedouin.

The economic prospects of the formerly impoverished Arabian Peninsula were transformed in 1938 with the first discovery of oil deposits at Dhahran. Now one-third of the world's reserves are known to be located here, close to the surface so they can be inexpensively retrieved, allowing the Arab states to control prices by adjusting supply and to meet world shortages

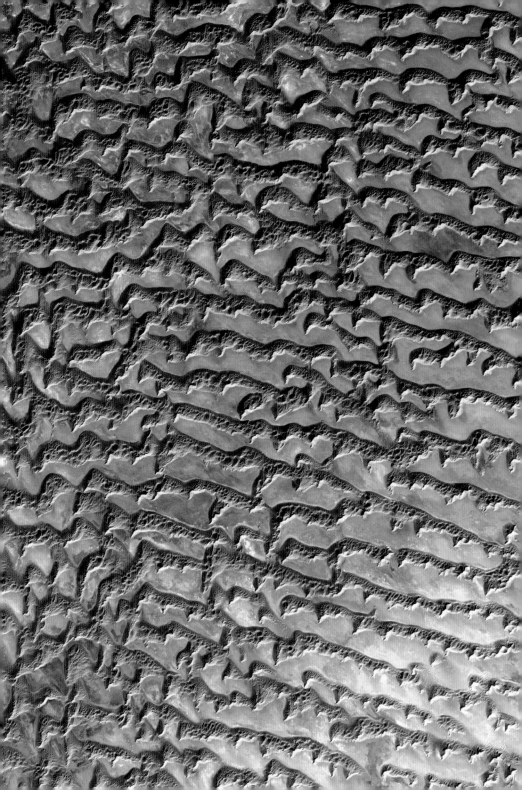

Kalahari Desert with characteristic thorn trees, 2003.

by increasing capacity. An even more valuable deposit is fossil water, accessible from Ice Age aquifers where it has been trapped for 25,000 years. However, draining these reservoirs for agriculture only increases salinity and becomes self-defeating.

Unlike these stereotypical deserts, the Kalahari (from the local Tswana *khalagari*, meaning 'waterless place'), which extends through most of Botswana into Namibia and South Africa, is not a true desert overall, since many regions have a rainfall exceeding 250 mm and the dunes are well vegetated. Its one permanent river, the Okavango, flows into an inland delta with extensive marshlands that attract large quantities of wildlife – and tourists to observe them. In the Kalahari Gemsbok National Park ancient riverbeds (*omuramba*) retain pools of water during the rainy season, supporting lions, wild dogs, jackals, meerkats and ostriches. Like many deserts it was once a fertile area, but the ancient Lake Makgadikgadi, which covered some 80,000 square km to a depth of 30 m, drained away 10,000 years ago and is now only a series of salt pans. Mining of coal and copper was the economic mainstay of the region until 1971, when the Debswana Diamond Mines, now the world's largest producer of gem diamonds, opened at Orapa in northern Botswana.

The Thar (from the Urdu *t'hul* or *dhool*, meaning 'sand'), or Great Indian Desert, between West Pakistan and northwestern

Satellite image of sand dunes in the Rub' al Khali, 2005.

India is the most highly populated desert in the world. Now characterized by sand dunes and wind-sculptured rocks, it was once watered by the Ghaggar river, which dried up in 2,000 BCE and now flows only intermittently. In the ancient Indian epic Ramayana this area, known in the story as Lavanasagara (the 'salt-ocean'), was formed when Rama threw his fire-bearing arrow into an ocean, which immediately dried up, becoming the Thar desert. Intriguingly, marine fossils have been found in its playas, or saline lakes, and archaeologists have recovered evidence of ancient habitations beneath them, confirming their antiquity.

Wahiba Sands, desert region of Oman, 2008.

The Rajasthan or Indira Gandhi Canal system, the major irrigation scheme of the Thar Desert, carries water 650 km from the north to the cities of Bikaner and Jaisalmer and provides power for Jodhpur and Bikaner. Irrigation has transformed this barren desert into fertile fields (the so-called 'green revolution') producing wheat, mustard and cotton; yet, as in many deserts, it has had damaging side-effects. The excessive irrigation needed for these water-intensive crops has produced a rising water table with increased salinity and land subsidence. Despite a tree-planting programme for dune stabilization, the Thar is spreading as high-velocity winds blow sand on to neighbouring fertile lands, producing shifting sand dunes and blocking roads and railway tracks.

Although they lie close together, the three North American hot deserts have very different characteristics. The largest, the Chihuahuan Desert, lies in the rain shadow of the Sierra Madre mountain chains in the USA and Mexico. Mountain ranges of up to 1,500 m make it cooler than latitude alone would suggest and the fertile valleys of the Rio Grande and the Pecos permit a diversity of plants and animals, particularly birds. In addition, long-term seepage has collected as sub-surface water, giving rise to oases, some of which, like the Cuatro Ciénegas Basin in Mexico, support fish and aquatic turtles, attracting snorkelling tourists.[3] The Chihuahuan is a relatively young desert, only 8,000 years old, and its character has changed even in the last 150 years. With more sophisticated technology the sub-surface water is now more easily accessed and supports increasing numbers of cattle; these have trampled and eaten the once prolific grasses, leading to a shrub invasion and increased desertification.

The Sonoran Desert in southwestern Arizona, California and Mexico is the hottest of the North American deserts. Unique to this desert are the California fan palm oases that grow around springs, resulting from activity along the San Andreas Fault.[4] Unfortunately, they are threatened by the depletion of aquifers resulting from urbanization and irrigation.

The Mojave Desert, named after the Mojave tribe of Native Americans, lies in the rain shadow of the Sierra Nevada Mountains

between the cold Great Basin Desert to the north and the hot Sonoran Desert to the south. The area around the Colorado River in the east is best known for its high mesas, plateaux and deep canyons, most famously the Colorado Canyon. Another striking feature is the golden pink Kelso Dunes, up to 180 m high, which are heard to 'sing' or 'boom' when the grains of rose quartz and feldspar rub against each other on the steep upper slopes. The smallest of the four North American deserts, it nevertheless contains the world's largest solar-array power plant and the much-photographed Death Valley, where temperatures soaring to 56.7°c have been recorded at Furnace Creek.

Australia is the world's driest inhabited continent; over 79 per cent of it is arid zone and 38 per cent desert. Nevertheless the arid areas experience extreme variability in rainfall as decades-long droughts may be followed by torrential rains. After a deluge

Kelso 'Singing' Sands, Mojave Desert, 2008.

most water evaporates quickly or runs into the sand, though clay pans hold water longer, and chains of waterholes, well known to the local Aboriginal people, are refilled. Sustained heavy rains replenish long-dry rivers and water moves slowly across the continent, recharging aquifers and underground rivers.

A striking feature of the Australian desert is the mirage-haunted Lake Eyre, which at 16 m below sea-level is known as the 'bath-plug of the continent'. For decades at a time this playa lake can be almost totally dry – a dazzling white salt pan hard enough to hold car racing events on.[5] Yet heavy monsoonal rains in Queensland, flowing down Cooper Creek, fill Lake Eyre to a depth of 4 m. The transformation is extreme. Brilliant flowers appear; the lake teems with fish and frogs; birds fly in from all directions for the feast; and tourists converge on the lake and its air space to observe this rare and short-lived event.

As well as extremes of rainfall, the Australian arid region is notable for its diverse landforms, textures and colours: the spectacular red sand dunes of the Simpson and Tanami Deserts; chains of mountains such as the ancient Petermann Ranges, thrust up 600 MYA, higher than the Himalayas but now eroded down; the MacDonnell Ranges that 310 MYA were more than 9 km high; the Musgraves, the Kimberleys and the Hammersleys, standing out like the ribs of an ancient carcass; the striated 'beehive' structures near Kings Canyon and in the Pilbara; extensive areas of woody shrubland; heavily vegetated river channels; open gibbers, or desert pavements, hard plains composed of rock and pebble; oases of rare plants, including ancient cycads; the brilliant-white coastal dunes of the Great Australian Bight and inland from them, on the northeast edge of the Nullarbor Plain, 35-million-year-old dunes, probably the oldest in the world, that mark the one-time coast of the continent; hot mound springs like Dalhousie Springs where the emerging water temperature is 43°C; salt lakes and clay pans with a thin crystalline skin or a surface of baked mud, fissured into chocolate-coloured plaques curling at the edges; and, most famously, the massive inselbergs, Uluru (Ayers Rock) and Mount Connor, rising abruptly from the desert plain. In Aboriginal culture this bountiful variety

of landforms is documented in minute detail so that even the smallest mound or declivity has, for the local people, a complex history and spiritual meaning.

Uluru at sunset, 2006.

Because of the great age of the Australian continent, its desert soils have been heavily leached and are deficient in nitrogen, phosphorus and trace elements, making them poor and unproductive. Yet these deserts, with their high climatic variability, have hosted a long evolutionary history that includes ancient plants, unique megafauna and a record of human occupation dating back some 50,000 years: the world's oldest continuing culture.

Six major hot deserts are found in Australia: the Great Victoria, the Great Sandy, the Tanami, the Simpson, the Gibson and Sturt Stony Desert. Crossing the Great Victoria Desert with camels in 1875, the explorer Ernest Giles was overcome by a sense of desolation, recording, 'It was totally uninhabited by either man or animal, not a track of a single marsupial, emu, or wild dog was to be seen and we seemed to have penetrated into a region utterly unknown to man, and as utterly forsaken by God.'[6]

During the Cretaceous Period the Great Sandy Desert was covered with forests of conifers and palms, with ferns and mosses flourishing beneath them. Now this desert in north-western Australia is characterized by large ergs with parallel sand dunes running West-northwest. The 1,850-km Canning Stock Route passes through this desert and the neighbouring Little Sandy Desert, relying on 48 wells sunk between 1908 and 1910 when captured Aboriginal *Martu* men were chained and hand-cuffed and forced, through thirst, to disclose the location of their precious 'soaks'.[7]

The Simpson Desert is one vast erg characterized by the spectacular deep-red colour of its quartz sand and by the world's longest parallel dunes. These are up to 200 km in length and approximately 500 m apart, and all run North-northwest to South-southeast because they are aligned with the dominant wind patterns of 20,000 years ago.[8] In 1845 the explorer Charles Sturt, the first European to encounter these dunes, wrote in desperation: 'Ascending one of the sand ridges I saw a numberless succession . . . rising above each other to the east and west . . . A kind of dread came over me . . . It looked like the entrance into Hell.'[9] Yet beneath the Simpson Desert lies the Great Artesian Basin, one of the world's largest inland drainage systems. Its underground water surfaces in natural springs and in bores sunk along the stock routes.

The Gibson Desert, lying along the Tropic of Capricorn, was named in 1874 by the explorer Ernest Giles, who trudged 100 km across this terrifying expanse carrying a keg of precious water after his companion Alfred Gibson, who had taken their only

The Simpson Desert, central Australia, 2012.

remaining horse to get help, disappeared. Giles noted the variable terrain: gravel areas supporting thin grasses, dunes, rocky ridges, sandy upland areas, saltwater lakes and spinifex that tormented men and horses alike with its sharp needles. Now large numbers of feral camels roam this area.

Cold Winter Deserts

The Gobi Desert (from the Mongolian *govi*, meaning 'waterless place' or 'semi-desert') is a cold desert plateau stretching in an arc across parts of northern and northwestern China and southern Mongolia. Despite its name, only the southwestern quarter of this desert is entirely without water, the remainder being covered with sparse vegetation. The area known as the Badain Jaran (meaning 'mysterious lakes') Desert contains star dunes up to 500 m high, the tallest stationary dunes in the world, but most of the Gobi is gravel or bare rock as high winds have stripped away the sand cover. This is another desert with extremes in temperature, soaring to 50°c in summer and plunging to −40°c in winter when fierce winds from the Siberian Steppes bring snow and icy sandstorms. Through desertification the Gobi is expanding each year into existing Chinese farmland, despite extensive tree-planting programmes intended to stabilize the dunes.

In the Nemegt Basin in Mongolia fossils of early mammals, dinosaur eggs and 100,000-year-old stone implements have been discovered. The theropod Deinocheirus, the fossilized forelegs of which were found in southern Mongolia, was probably the fastest and largest dinosaur ever to exist. In 2001 palaeontologists unearthed a 90-million-year-old graveyard of more than a dozen juvenile, ostrich-like dinosaurs (ornithomimosaurs), all of which had apparently been trapped in mud at the same time, suggesting that bands of juveniles may have roamed separately from the adults.[10] Huge deposits of gold and copper have recently been found at Oyu Tolgoi in Mongolia; the Rio Tinto company expects that its mining operations there will increase the country's gross domestic product by one-third by 2020 and be viable for more than 50 years.[11]

'Booming' star-dunes in the Badain Jaran Desert, part of the Gobi desert, Mongolia.

The Patagonian Desert, the largest in the Americas, is located mainly in Argentina and extends into Chile. Lying in the rain shadow of the Andes, it is further desiccated by the effects of the cold Falkland current off the Atlantic coast. Before the up-thrust of the Andes, ash from nearby volcanoes blanketed the temperate forests that covered the area, leaving the world's most extensive petrified forests in the centre of what is now desert. Covered by gravel plains, much of Patagonia is bleak and arid, yet it fascinated Charles Darwin, who wrote:

> They [the plains of Patagonia] can be described only by negative characteristics; without habitations, without water, without trees, without mountains, they support merely a few dwarf plants. Why then . . . have these arid wastes taken so firm a hold on my memory? . . . it must be partly owing to the free scope given to the imagination.[12]

The Karakum Desert (also Kara Kum, from the Turkmen *gara gum*, meaning 'Black Sand') covers about 90 per cent of Turkmenistan between the Caspian and Aral seas. Its climate is classically continental, ranging from 34°c to −20°c, but there is little snow because of the minimal precipitation, rainfall being registered only about once in a decade. Yet 30 MYA this desert was covered by sea before mountain upthrusts in the south diminished it, leaving only the Amu Darya river flowing across the Karakum. Violent winds have erected towering sand ridges up to 90 m high and crescent-shaped dunes or barchans. The desert is now crossed by the 1,375-kilometre Karakum Canal, the largest irrigation canal in the world. Begun in 1954, it has greatly increased productivity but has also led to secondary salinization of the soil, forming a salt crust that requires new drainage systems to divert the salts away from cultivated areas.

Despite its current aridity and sparse population (one person per 6.5 square km), Russian archaeologists have found evidence of Stone and Bronze Age cultures in the Anau and Dzheytun regions. The latter is possibly the earliest agricultural settlement in western Central Asia, as canals dating from the third millennium BCE have been discovered around Geoksyur.[13]

The Kyzyl Kum desert (from Uzbek *qizilqum*, meaning 'red sand') extending through Kazakhstan, Uzbekistan and part of Turkmenistan is an elevated plain comprising rocky areas with shifting sand dunes and sparse vegetation, the river valleys of the Amu Darya and Syr Darya, the landlocked Aral Sea and scattered oases. The Kyzyl Kum has rich deposits of gold, uranium, copper, aluminium, silver, natural gas and oil. In Uzbekistan diverse fossils from the late Cretaceous Period have been found – early bird species, crocodylomorphs, turtles, various dinosaur species

Skull of the *Probactrosaurus gobiensis* dinosaur, Paleozoological Museum of China, Beijing.

Satellite image of an alluvial fan formed by the Molcha River as it leaves the Altyn-Tagh mountains and enters the southern part of the Taklamakan Desert, northwest China. The photo was taken in May, when the river is full with snow and glacier meltwater, 2002.

including ostrich-like dinosaurs (ornithomimosaurs) and horned dinosaurs,[14] and small early mammals.

West of the Gobi, in the Tarim Basin of northwest China, lies the Taklamakan Desert (the name is probably the Uyghur version of the Arabic for 'to leave alone' or 'relinquish' + 'place'). A classical cold, sandy desert, it is surrounded by mountain ranges on three sides – the Kunlun Mountains to the south, the Pamirs to the west and the Tien Shan or Heavenly Mountains to the north. To the northeast is the Turfan (or Turpan) Depression, 155 m below sea level, the second-deepest hollow in the Earth's land surface. Rivers flow from the Kun Lun Mountains some 60 km into the desert, forming vast alluvial fans before drying up in

Snow blanketing Snake Valley and Wheeler Park in the Great Basin Desert, the coldest of the North American deserts, 2009.

the sand. The largest crescentic dunes in the world, over 3 km apart, are in the Taklamakan. Strong winds have also piled sand into pyramidal star dunes up to 1,000 m high; these raise dust clouds 4,000 m high, blanketing the Taklamakan for most of the year.[15] A *karaburan* or 'black hurricane' can engulf and bury an entire caravan. Like the Gobi, the Taklamakan receives frigid air masses from Siberia in winter that drive temperatures down to −20°c, causing rivers to freeze and frosting the sand dunes with snow.

Travellers on the Silk Road caravan route connecting China with Central Asia and Europe avoided this dangerous desert, following instead the line of oasis towns to the north or the south, but archaeological finds indicate that the Taklamakan has been a bi-directional highway for many races for much longer than recorded history.

The Great Basin Desert of North America, lying in the rain shadow of the Sierra Nevada and with an elevation of 1,000 m, is also a cold inland desert. Unlike the three neighbouring hot deserts discussed above, it is blanketed in snow in winter.

Cool Coastal Deserts

The Atacama Desert, lying in the rain shadow of the Andes, is the longest, driest and highest strip of arid land in the world, stretching nearly 3,000 km along the Pacific coast of South America from northern Peru to northern Chile and rising sharply to the arid Puna and Altiplano 1,000 m up in the Andes.[16] As well as vast expanses of desolation, there are diverse and spectacular landscapes: five snow-covered volcanoes, including Ojos del Salado (6,887 m), the highest in the world, lava flows, geysers, sand dunes, salt flats, turquoise lakes, the moon-like scenery of the Valle de la Luna and Valle de Muerte, and everywhere the dramatic backdrop of the Andes.

The average annual rainfall of the Atacama is 1.3 mm, but in some regions no rain has been recorded in the 400 years since the Spanish arrived; it may be that it has not rained in those areas for 20 million years.[17] Here decomposition does not occur, so dead vegetation may be thousands of years old. The only significant moisture comes from the dense fog formed when warm air from the Pacific is cooled by the cold air associated with the Humboldt or Peru Current originating in the Antarctic. In winter the fog is driven up the hills and falls as rain, producing areas of seasonal vegetation that allow animals to survive here. Rare thunderstorms drop rain on restricted areas, causing long-dormant seeds to germinate and bloom briefly.

Astrobiologists are studying the Atacama for clues about life on other dry planets and the conditions necessary for survival there. In a region south of Antofagasta the soil appears similar to that on Mars. Indeed, the Atacama was used as a location for filming 'Martian' scenes in the television series *Space Odyssey: Voyage to the Planets* (2004). It was long thought that the Atacaman soil contained no signs of even microbial life but in 2011 an 'oasis' of microorganisms was detected 2 m below the surface in hypersaline substrates. These primitive microorganisms (archaea and bacteria) grow without oxygen or sunlight, attracting the minimal

Camel thorn tree (*Acacia erioloba*) in Sossusvlei region, Namib-Naukluft National Park, Namib Desert, 2004.

Valle de la Luna, San Pedro, Chile, 2004.

moisture from the air and condensing it on salt crystals,[18] suggesting that similar microorganisms might exist on Mars or could be grown there.

The Namib (meaning 'vast area' in the Nama language) stretches for 1,600 km along the coast of Namibia and into southern Angola. Occupying a comparable position to the Atacama on the other side of the world, its aridity is maintained by the effect of the northward-flowing Benguela current converging with hot, dry winds from the land.[19] Rainfall is sparse and unpredictable and the main source of surface water is condensation of ocean fog, which is blown inland as far as 50 km in the central and northern Namib. The shifting dunes of the southern Namib, up to 300 m high and stretching to 320 km, have been carved by the prevailing southerly winds, leaving spectacular knife-edge ridges that are often crescent-shaped.

The Namib is the world's most ancient desert, being at least 55 million years old.[20] Some parts of it have been arid for at least 80 million years, since the glaciation of the Antarctic, and possibly for 130 million to 145 million years, since the continental split of West Gondwana.[21] Its main economic resource is diamond mining, though land-based production of the gems is now surpassed by marine diamond recovery from the seabed, which is calculated to contain some 2 billion carats.[22] Uranium, too, is mined in the Erongo region at the Rössing Uranium Mine, one of the largest open-pit uranium mines in the world and currently the sixth-largest producer of yellowcake.

Polar Deserts

By far the world's largest desert is Antarctica, with an area of 14,000,000 square km in summer and almost double that in winter, when sea ice forms around the coasts.[23] It is also the driest, windiest, coldest and most formidable desert in the world. When cold, dense air rolls off the 2,000 m ice plateau, powerful katabatic winds sweep the continent with gusts of up to 327 km per hour. The explorer Douglas Mawson called his account of Antarctica *The Home of the Blizzard* (1915), and recorded that in order to remain upright there, one must lean against the wind at an angle of 45 degrees. Antarctica is so cold partly because its ice sheet is up to 4 km thick; partly because the ice and snow reflect 80 per cent of solar radiation back to space and much of the remaining 20 per cent is reflected by clouds; and partly because it is isolated by the Southern Ocean from the rest of the Earth's weather systems. The lowest temperature ever recorded there was −89.2°c, at the Russian Vostok Station in 1983.

Beneath the continental ice shelf is solid land, recalling a time, 180 MYA, when Antarctica was neither so cold nor a desert, but joined to the other southern land masses as part of the megacontinent Gondwana. It sustained the tundra and extensive forests that produced coal and fossilized wood deposits and probably oil and natural gas reserves, and where dinosaurs and, later, marsupial mammals roamed the Antarctic Peninsula.[24] Indeed, the calculated age of the remains of southern beech (*Nothofagus*) suggests that the modern environment of Antarctica may be only 2–3 million years old.[25]

The continent is divided by the Transantarctic Mountains and has several dormant volcanoes, notably Mt Terror on Ross Island, and two active volcanoes: Mt Erebus, which has a permanent

molten lava lake, and one on Deception Island. Volcanic eruptions have been common in Antarctica over the last 25 million years, and recently a string of twelve volcanoes, seven of them active, and some rising 3,000 m above the ocean floor, has been mapped in the seas surrounding Antarctica.[26]

Aerial view of the main crater of Mt Erebus, Antarctica's active volcano, 2010.

When not obscured by blizzards, this vast, white wilderness is full of colour: deep-blue ice cliffs and glaciers, turquoise crevasses and caverns, and towering icebergs, their blue, green or striated ice reflected in calm water. Antarctica also provides the spectacle of the aurora australis or Southern Lights, visible only at latitudes higher than −40°. When this phenomenon is at its most brilliant, beams of coloured light like searchlights, coloured streamers or shimmering 'curtains', usually pink, red, green, blue or orange, light up the sky. The colours are caused by charged particles streaming from the sun at times of intense solar activity. Trapped by the Earth's magnetic field, they flow towards the Magnetic Poles. When they collide with gases in the upper atmosphere, they cause them to glow like neon tubes with vibrant colours.[27]

Because there were no indigenous people in Antarctica, it was the first and only continent to be 'discovered'. Now it is visited by thousands of tourists in the summer, and thousands more are attached to the research bases which have made the continent a giant laboratory for almost every science from microbiology to astronomy, geology, meteorology, botany, palaeontology, ecology and oceanography. There is grave concern that Antarctica is warming, though the causes of this are debated. In 2002 the Larsen-B ice shelf of the Antarctic Peninsula collapsed and in 2008 a large section of the Wilkins Ice Shelf also detached from the Peninsula. Significant warming extends beyond the Peninsula to most of West Antarctica, where the ice temperature has increased by more than 0.1°c per decade over the last 50 years.[28] The implications of a warmer Antarctica are enormous and cataclysmic. The ice and snow covering 98 per cent of the continent account for 70 per cent of the Earth's fresh water, so if its ice sheets melted, as large areas of the Arctic ice are already doing, the world's oceans would rise by 60–65 metres, inundating islands and coastal

Blue ice covering Lake Fryxell in the Transantarctic Mountains, Antarctica, 2002. The ice comes from glacier meltwater from the Canada Glacier and other smaller glaciers.

Aurora australis
with the South
Pole Telescope
in the foreground.

areas worldwide. The loss of life and the swelling of refugee numbers, with all the political and economic issues entailed, are incalculable.

While the geographical features of deserts are intriguing and pose many of the most urgent environmental questions of our time, for most readers the animals and the cultures that survive under such stringent conditions are of more immediate interest.

2 An Armoury of Adaptations

From so simple a beginning endless forms most beautiful and most wonderful have been, and are being, evolved.

Charles Darwin, *On the Origin of Species* (1859)

A trip to the desert in a four-wheel-drive vehicle is an exciting adventure, but a large, if unacknowledged, part of its attraction is being able to leave at will. To most of us it would seem impossible to live permanently in such conditions. Yet hundreds of species of plants and animals have evolved a fascinating armoury of adaptations that allow them to survive in conditions of extreme aridity, heat or cold. In investigating these many ingenious developments we look first at the ways plants conserve water, then at the ways animals accommodate to extremes of heat, cold and aridity.

Plants

Desert flora are xerophytic (that is, they need very little water) and often halophytic (salt-tolerant), since evaporating pools become progressively more saline. Xerophytes survive because the reduced number, size, shape or orientation of their leaves allows them to save, store or capture water. Alternatively they may remain dormant until rain arrives, then hasten through their life cycle in minimal time. These are the ephemerals that transform the desert into a garden.

The best-known water savers are the cacti, which dominate and are unique to North American deserts, providing the obligatory scenery for westerns. They have a battery of adaptations to drought, which are effective so long as there are also regular periods of rain. Reduction of leaves to spines reduces water loss

Boab tree, Timber Creek, Northern Territory, Australia, 2007.

by transpiration, breaks up air currents that promote evaporation and minimizes absorption of solar radiation. Their spines, along with the bitter taste of cactus 'juice', also deter thirsty herbivores. Their shallow root systems, which spread laterally to capture surface water, exist in a suspended state until activated by rain to produce fast-growing, temporary feeder roots. A thick, waxy cuticle, sometimes supplemented by matted hairs, insulates the plant from heat and further minimizes transpiration, while the bluish 'glaucous bloom' of the cuticle also helps reduce evaporation. Cactus stomata, which allow exchange of gases with the atmosphere, can close more tightly than in other plants, reducing moisture loss in the hottest part of the day. Their ribbed surface channels water, including condensation from dew or fog, down to the roots and acts as an accordion-like structure: when the plant's water is depleted, the 'pleats' close up, exposing less surface area to the sun, but when water is available they expand to accommodate it in the cell vacuoles. A dehydrated cactus droops, reducing exposure to the sun and shading the lower parts of the plant. The wide, flat, waxy pads of some cacti transpire little water and have a protein structure that is stable at relatively high temperatures.

Cholla cactus in bloom, Mojave Desert.

Saguaro cactus in Arizona, 2005; the man in the photo is 1.55 m (5 ft) tall.

The giant, column-like saguaro cactus (*Carnegiea gigantea*), unique to the Sonoran Desert, is the largest and most striking of all cacti, growing to a height of 12–18 m and, when fully hydrated, weighing up to 2,100 kg. Saguaros grow very slowly (a ten-year-old plant may be only 10–15 cm tall) but live for up to 200 years, producing side branches that bend upwards. Their white flowers and red fruit, highly visible in open spaces, attract birds for seed dispersal. Other cacti, too, have succeeded in this eco-region – the cholla (*Cylindropuntia*), the organ pipe (*Lemaireocereus*), the silver dollar cactus or prickly pear (*Opuntia robusta*) and the jojoba (*Simmondsia chinensis*).

Lithops salicola, native to southern Africa.

In Australian deserts, where drought may last for a decade, cacti are rare. Equivalent water storers are boab trees (*Adansonia gregorii*), which are related to the Madagascan and African *Adansonia* species known as baobabs. These plants, which can live to 1,500 years, store water in their trunks, giving them a distinctive bottle shape with a girth of up to 20 m. In dry seasons boabs drop their leaves to conserve water, but new leaves sprout just before the wet season approaches.

Leaf modifications provide other means of conserving water. Thick hairs on the small, succulent leaves of saltbush (*Atriplex* sp.), the main scrubby species in arid Australia, prevent wind evaporation and their grey-green or blue-green colour reflects sunlight, while shallow, wide-spreading roots soak up any moisture over a large area. Saltbush tolerates high salt levels by secreting salt on to the leaf surface to balance osmotic pressure, retain water and reflect sunlight to cool it.

The intriguing lithops (*Lithops* sp.) plants of the Namib and Kalahari deserts look exactly like a pair of rounded pebbles lying on the ground, providing excellent camouflage protection from grazing animals. The plant has hardly any stem, its main part being a pair of bulbous leaves mostly buried beneath the ground to conserve water, with a partly or completely translucent top surface that allows light to enter for photosynthesis.

The most characteristic grasses of the Australian deserts are the 64 endemic species of spinifex (*Triodia* sp.) that grow on the slopes of dunes and the corridors between them, comprising half the ground cover and approximately 96 per cent of the biomass in these areas. *Triodia* grows as an expanding dome. The young green leaves on the outer edge of the hummock are flat and relatively soft, but their edges roll inwards as they age to produce a stiff, pointed, spear-like leaf. The centre of the hummock becomes a mass of matted stems and dead leaves up to 1.2 m wide and 60 cm high, and eventually collapses, leaving a ring of new leaves. This closely packed hummock grass generates its own microclimate, minimizing temperature fluctuations, providing internal shade and reducing evaporation in the heat of the day while retaining warm air on cold nights. The silvery surface of the leaves reflects sunlight, reducing water loss. A much sought-after refuge for small animals, it also provides a food source for numerous insects that in turn support reptiles, mammals and birds. Additionally its roots

Spinifex grass (*Triodia*).

Joshua trees (*Yucca brevifolia*) at sunrise in Joshua Tree National Park, California, 2008.

compact the sand, allowing animals to burrow without the sand collapsing on them.

Unlike the shallow-rooted cacti and saltbush, phreatophytes have root systems long enough to reach water sources deep underground. The sagebrush (*Artemisia tridentata*) sends roots down 25 m, drawing in water throughout the summer. The Joshua tree (*Yucca brevifolia*), unique to the Mojave Desert, has a deep and extensive root system that reaches out 11 m.[1] Joshua trees produce flowers and seeds only after sufficient rainfall at the right season; in times of severe drought, they instead produce new stems from underground rhizomes.

The longest known taproot system is that of the mesquite bush (*Prosopis* sp.) of the Sonoran and Chihuahuan deserts. Reaching down 58 m, it enables the plant to draw from a deep water table as well as to access surface water when available.[2] The nara melon (or !nara, *Acanthosicyos horridus*), which grows in coastal areas of the Namib Desert near dry riverbeds, also has a long taproot that penetrates deep into the sand in search of water.[3] Fossil evidence suggests that this species has existed for 40 million years, half the age of the Namib itself.

The most successful of the Australian phreatophytes is mulga (*Acacia aneura*), which covers about one-third of the entire arid zone and includes some 800 species. Mulgas have a 3-m-deep taproot and, after the seedling stage, most have their leaves replaced by phyllodes – flattened leaf stalks with parallel veins – to minimize moisture loss.[4] The leaves and branches of the horse mulga (*Acacia ramulosa*) direct water towards the trunk, where it trickles down to the dense roots that suck it up before it drains into the desert soil. This process is so efficient that a 5-m shrub can collect 100 litres of water from a 12-mm rain shower.

An unusual adaptation to aridity is that of welwitschia (*Welwitschia mirabilis*), a unique conifer that, like flowering plants, is pollinated by beetles and insects and can live for more than 1,000 years in the barren sand dunes of the eastern Namib.[5] Its far-reaching taproot reaches deep underground and is capable of storing water, but welwitschia also traps another source of moisture – the fog that blows intermittently from the Atlantic. The plant absorbs condensed fog through the pores of its 2-m-wide leaves, which can grow to almost 10 m in length.

Plants of the Atacama Desert on the west coast of South America have also evolved to profit from the ephemeral microclimate provided by fog rolling in from the coast: hypolithic algae, lichens, numerous species of the bromeliad *Tillandsia*, *Deuterocohnia chrysantha*, *Puya boliviensis* and cacti with thorns all trap condensing fog droplets.[6] Desert tillandsias can also absorb humidity from the air through the trichomes (hairs) on their leaves. Other fog-zone plant communities have evolved in transient 'fog oases' where mountains or steep coastal slopes and gorges trap clouds. Short-lived perennials and scrubby vegetation grow there briefly in the winter, hosting migratory birds such as the Peruvian song-sparrow, the Pacific blue-black grassquit and hummingbirds for at least part of the year.

The seeds of some plants can remain dormant for years, even decades, of drought, but after rain they germinate and bloom in a few hours. Such ephemerals usually bear brilliantly coloured flowers to attract insects for rapid pollination, since the whole reproductive cycle has to be completed before the moisture dries up. In the Australian deserts the blazing red flowers of Sturt's desert pea (*Swainsona formosus*), bright pink parakeelya (*Calandrinia polyandra*), brilliant yellow billy buttons (*Craspedia globosa*) and *Senna glutinosa* appear within days after rain, and paper daisies (*Helichrysum*) carpet the ground. The artist and naturalist Charles McCubbin (1930–2010), on first seeing the desert after rain, wrote, 'Nothing prepared us for the vast exuberant flower garden that filled the middle desert. Mile after mile of blooms – a great incredible sea of flowers that flowed between the dunes and splashed their slopes in yellow, white, pink and gold.'[7] Ephemerals disperse their seeds rapidly in a variety of ways. Some rely on animals to carry them; some have miniature

Welwitschia mirabilis, approximately 1,500 years old, unique to the Namib Desert.

Sturt's desert pea
(*Swainsona formosa*).

parachutes to facilitate wind dispersal; others have explosive devices
to spray out seeds as the pod dries.

As protection against temporary environmental changes,
some seeds have built-in sensors that respond to specific levels of
water, temperature and light to prevent premature germination
after a mere passing shower. Several Australian desert plants have
seeds with an extremely hard outer coating that requires scratch-
ing or fire to germinate. Desert fuchsias (*Eremophila latrobei*)
produce hard seed cases that germinate only after fire and rain.[8]

Indeed, as was well known to Aboriginal Australians, fire is essential in regulating the diversity and abundance of species present in particular areas at specific stages of their life cycle.

Animals

The fauna of most deserts are diverse, unique and often hidden from the casual observer. They survive the harsh conditions in a variety of ways, many analogous to those of plants. Some derive sufficient water from ingested food; some conserve water by excreting highly concentrated urine; others store quantities of food as fat, as camels famously do. They may avoid water loss through evaporation by remaining underground during the heat of the day and emerging at dusk or at night to hunt or scavenge. Some defer reproduction until conditions are favourable. We look now at the some of these ingenious survival strategies across the range of animal phyla that inhabit desert terrains.

In the world's driest desert after Antarctica, the Atacama, fauna are almost non-existent. Even bacteria are scarce and in many parts insects are absent.[9] However, in other deserts (with the exception of Antarctica) insects are plentiful. The architectural feats of the humble termite are the most conspicuous of the insect adaptations. Since their eggs require strict temperature control to within 1°c of optimum, termites in the Northern Territory of Australia, often wrongly called 'white ants' (they are related to cockroaches, not ants), erect extraordinary edifices to regulate the temperature of the networks of tunnels, arches and nursery chambers within. These are of two kinds: giant 'cathedral' mounds that tower 4 m above the ground and thin 'magnetic' mounds that are up to 2 m high. The latter are aligned with their long axis running north to south and their broad sides facing east and west. This permits the smallest possible surface to be exposed to the midday sun while allowing the eastern face to be warmed in the morning, followed by a plateau in temperature until sunset. The column of warm air rising out of the mound produces circulation currents throughout the network. During the winter season large numbers of termites, including workers, larvae and reproductive nymphs, move in the morning to the eastern face, which warms first, and remain there during the day.[10] In Africa some termites cultivate indoor fungi gardens, which also require strictly controlled temperature within the mounds.

Australian mulga ants (*Polyrhachis macropa*) surround the entrance to their underground chambers with a cylindrical wall of soil and a palisade of twigs to act as a levee bank against sudden flooding. Often the whole construction is also thatched with mulga to prevent erosion. Harvester ants in the Colorado Desert insulate their mounds with tiny 'rocks', some of which are the

Termite cathedral mound in Northern Territory, Australia.

fossilized teeth of fish, including sharks – evidence that this desert was once an ancient sea.[11]

Beetles can survive on very little water but in the Namib even that little must be painstakingly collected. In an amazing evolutionary adaptation, the Namib desert beetle *Stenocara gracilipes*, which lives in the coastal dunes, collects its supply of moisture from the fog that rolls in intermittently but rapidly at 16 km per hour from the Atlantic. The beetle hastens to the top of a sand ridge and faces into the wind, spreading its wings, straightening out its rear legs and lowering its head to make a 45° angle. Fog vapour collects on its wings and coalesces to form water droplets that roll down the beetle's back to its mouth. Namib fog travels so fast that it will not stick to or condense on most surfaces, but *Stenocara*'s back is exceptionally efficient in water capture: it combines hydrophilic ridges with waxy hydrophobic furrows that funnel water to its mouth. This elegant 'design' is being copied to make more efficient fog nets for people in the Atacama and to devise more effective dehumidifiers and distillation equipment worldwide.[12]

Lepidochora beetles also depend on the fog of the Namib Desert for water and survival. They live in the coastal sand dunes, where each morning they build tiny raised sand ridges perpendicular to the flow of the fog-bearing winds. As these constructions intercept the incoming fog, the beetles creep along them, sucking up the condensation.

Arachnids, which include scorpions, ticks and spiders, are also well adapted to desert life. One of the largest and most aggressive of spiders in the Australian desert is the hairy barking spider (*Selenocosmia stirlingi*), which measures at least 12 cm across. It roams to forage as well as building a fishing-line mesh around its open-holed burrow. Sudden sheet flooding is a hazard for desert spiders and many also construct a 'bath-plug' door to waterproof their underground nests.

Crustaceans are not normally prolific in deserts but some, like the tiny shield shrimp (*Triops*), survive in the Australian deserts because of their ability to tolerate high levels of salinity. In puddles and lakes formed on clay pans after heavy rain, shield

'Fog beetle', *Stenocara gracilipes*, at Epupa Falls, Namibia.

shrimps grow almost as you watch from tough, resistant eggs to 1.5-cm-long shrimps, but their lives are a race against time as the water rapidly evaporates. By the twelfth day, when the female shrimps are about 3 cm long, hundreds of tiny eggs have formed on their underbodies and are laid in the last remaining patch of damp soil. The adults die as the water turns to thick mud but the eggs remain dormant, for many years if necessary, awaiting the next rains.

Desert environments present great difficulties for amphibians that spend at least part of their life cycles in water. Tiger salamanders (*Ambystoma tigrinum*) enter the Sonoran desert only near permanent ponds, streams or springs and can remain in their larval state for their entire lives, even reproducing as such, and only rarely metamorphosing into terrestrial adults. Sonoran desert toads, desert spadefoots, tree frogs and others have hardened 'spades' on their hind feet for digging and survive in the desert by excavating metre-deep burrows where they spend nine or ten months at a time. Within their burrows, spadefoots secrete a semi-permeable membrane that thickens their skins and prevents water loss. They also have a high urea tolerance, since they do not excrete urine while in the burrow. The challenge for desert amphibians is to complete their reproduction in the temporary pools produced by sporadic and localized summer thunderstorms before they dry up again. Desert spadefoots (*Notaden nichollsi*) have evolved an accelerated development rate – from egg to toadlet in less than two weeks. In southeastern California, where summer rainfall is at its least reliable, spadefoots often emerge during the first storm, travel to ponds, breed and gorge on lipid-rich, swarming termites in a single night.[13]

In the Australian desert there are some twenty species of water-retaining, burrowing frogs whose broad heads and short limbs with digging structures on the underside of their feet make them efficient excavating machines. They can also literally absorb water from moist ground by flattening themselves out so that negative pressure between the cells of the ventral skin 'blots' up water. Like their American counterparts, they can produce an external cocoon of old, dead skin that remains around the body like plastic wrap, conserving water. Their burrows are so deep that only heavy rainfall percolates down to wake them up for breeding, but once that happens they mate rapidly and the development from egg to tadpole to frog is accelerated by voracious feeding.[14] Unlike the puddle-seeking frogs, the tiny sandhill frog (*Arenophryne rotunda*) of Western Australia lives and breeds deep in sandhills. Mating pairs of frogs burrow down frontwards as the moisture level falls but emerge at night to feed. Uniquely, the sandhill frog has no tadpole stage: instead tiny adult frogs emerge directly from the eggs after ten weeks.[15]

Central Australia has the greatest diversity of reptiles of any habitat in the world, with up to 40 species coexisting per square kilometre. Lizards in particular – from the largest Australian lizard and second-largest in the world, *Varanus giganteus*, at 2 m long, to tiny skinks – have adapted to these dry areas. Being cold-blooded, they can tolerate a wide range of temperatures. Nevertheless, some lizards burrow to avoid water loss; some climb; some take cover under rocks or grass hummocks; and others seek open spaces. Lizards forage in all shifts around the clock, so different species can coexist in a particular area by partitioning space, the times of day when they are active and the types of prey they devour. Skinks (*Ctenotus*) have adapted perfectly to the spinifex ecosystem,[16]

Perentie monitor lizard
(*Varanus giganteus*).

and can live in close proximity to each other because of their diverse use of their habitat and hunting times.

The fearsome-looking Australian thorny devil (*Moloch horridus*), studded with spines and tubercles, is actually harmless to all but the small black ants it devours at a rate of 5,000 a day. Its tough, spiked skin minimizes evaporation and provides insulation, changing colour depending on the temperature. It has also evolved a unique means of acquiring water. Between the scales of its skin is a network of narrow grooves that channel moisture by capillary action from the soil to the corners of its mouth. In addition, its fierce-looking conical spines, 15 cm long, are not just a deterrent to enemies but maximize the surface for condensation of vapour or dew, which is also drawn along capillary-like channels to the mouth.[17]

Geckos (for example, *Nephrurus levis*) effectively drink from their large, bulbous eyes, which have no eyelids but collect condensing dew on a transparent membrane. The gecko licks this by flicking its long tongue across its face.

Thorny devil (*Moloch horridus*), Western Australia.

Mojave Desert tortoises (*Gopherus agassizii*) also have an array of adaptations enabling them to survive in desert environments where temperatures can reach 60°c. With their thick, strong legs and well-developed claws, they dig underground burrows to escape the heat of the day, emerging only in the morning or late afternoon to forage. They also hibernate, venturing out only during winter storms to replenish their water stores. They may dig shallow basins in impermeable soil to catch rainwater but, equally, they may go for many years without drinking by feeding in spring on plants that provide them with sufficient water for the year. A Mojave tortoise can hold an impressive 1.2 litres of water in its bladder (twice the human capacity) and exist for a year without water.[18] They are triumphant survivors, living for 80 to 100 years in this extreme environment.

The easiest way to survive a lack of water may be to leave the area, and many bird species that live in desert regions migrate to avoid harsh conditions, returning in good seasons. Many will breed only after significant rainfall and when there is enough food for their young. In the Australian deserts tiny budgerigars (*Melopsittacus undulatus*) travel hundreds, even thousands, of kilometres when conditions become too dry. Desert birds have also developed behavioural strategies to reduce the effects of heat and evaporation: they rest during the hottest part of the day, flying to water to drink during the cool of the morning or late afternoon; refrain from fighting other birds; and maintain long-lasting bonds between pairs to avoid expending energy on elaborate mating displays.

During times of drought, Australian water birds such as pelicans flock to salt lakes, mound springs and permanently flowing bores. Seasonal wetlands within the Kalahari, such as the Makgadikgadi Pans of Botswana, similarly support numerous halophilic (salt-loving) species; in the rainy season, tens of thousands of flamingos visit the area. Even in the Atacama flocks of flamingos live in and around the salt lakes, feeding on the red algae that grow in them.

The best known of all desert dwellers, and an essential element of the Western stereotype of the desert, is the dromedary camel. Camels have a formidable range of adaptations that enable them

Desert tortoise (*Gopherus agassizii*) photographed in the Mojave Desert.

Dromedary (*Camelus dromedarius*).

to survive hot, dry days and cold nights. They conserve water by producing very dry faeces in tiny cubes and highly concentrated urine. They can survive an increase in body temperature to 45 °C, a temperature that would kill most mammals. Thus they do not need to sweat to keep cool and so can retain more water. They can lose up to 25 per cent of their body weight through water loss and rehydrate rapidly as soon as water is available. A severely dehydrated camel may drink up to 150 litres of water in ten minutes – roughly the same rate as filling a car with petrol. They can drink salty water without being sick and store fat in their humps to survive long periods without food. Their deeply recessed eyes are shaded from the sun and protected from dust and flying sand by long, thick eyelashes; inside their ears, thick hair serves the same purpose. Their nostrils are slits that can be folded down to conserve moisture when they exhale and as protection against sand storms. Their thick coats of rough fur and the under-wool on their backs provide insulation from both cold desert nights and the burning midday sun, while dense pads on elbows and knees bear the animal's weight when it sits. A web of skin between its toes prevents it from sinking into the sand, even when carrying heavy loads. Some of these characteristics are present in other mammals but none has the camel's range of adaptations.

Another Saharan animal, the fennec fox (*Vulpes zerda*), at only 20 cm tall the smallest of the fox family, is a nocturnal hunter of rodents, insects, birds and eggs that burrows underground in the heat of the day.[19] Like the camel, it can go without drinking for long periods and excretes concentrated urine to preserve water, while furry soles protect its feet from the burning sand. Its disproportionately large ears (15 cm long) dissipate heat as well as allowing it to hear prey from a great distance. A parallel adaptation is seen in the long ears of jackrabbits (actually hares) in North American deserts. The black-tailed jackrabbit (*Lepus californicus*) and the antelope jackrabbit (*Lepus alleni*) have paper-thin ears that are complex thermoregulators for the body, losing heat by dilation of the blood vessels to bring them nearer the skin's surface and reflecting light from surface hairs. These nocturnal

Fennec foxes
(*Vulpes zerda*).

feeders acquire all their water needs from the plants they eat. The gemsbok (*Oryx gazella*) of the Kalahari also conserves water by not sweating. Its body temperature can spiral to 45°c but it survives by dint of a blood-cooling circulation network in its nose, which keeps its brain cool.

Sheltering from the heat of the day is a common adaptation to minimize water loss in hot deserts. The endangered Northwest African cheetah (*Acinonyx jubatus hecki*), found mainly in the Sahara, is almost totally nocturnal,[20] and many Australian desert animals shelter underground or in clumps of vegetation such as spinifex, feeding at dusk. The bilby (*Macrotis lagotis*), many varieties of marsupial mouse such as mulgara (*Dasycercus cristicauda*), dunnarts (*Sminthopsis* genus) and spinifex hopping

Gemsbok (*Oryx gazella*) with helmeted guineafowl (*Numida meleagris*) at Chudop waterhole, Etosha, Namibia.

Jackrabbit (*Lepus* genus).

mice (*Notomys alexis*) are all crepuscular (dusk) feeders, as are red kangaroos (*Macropus rufus*) and the rufous hare wallaby (*Lagorchestes hirsutus*).

Many of these animals have additional biological adaptations to conserve water. Dasyurids, Australian carnivorous marsupials comprising dunnarts, the Pilbara ningaui (*N. timealeyi*) and the mulgara, rarely need to drink because the insects, spiders (a favourite food of all of these is the juicy barking spider), grasshoppers and small vertebrates they eat contain about 60 per cent water. They also avoid heat stress by hunting at night and hiding in the spinifex during the day. In times of plenty dasyurids also store fat around their tails to be reabsorbed when needed. Since insects are plentiful throughout the year, they can breed seasonally regardless of drought.

The red kangaroo, the largest surviving marsupial, is well adapted to aridity. Kangaroos are extremely mobile, leaping 5 m in one bound. At high speeds, such hopping on two legs is more efficient than running on all fours because the Achilles tendon in each hind leg acts like a spring, recycling energy with every bound. Whereas a four-legged animal uses more energy to go faster, the kangaroo simply lengthens its stride while using the same hopping frequency. In addition, as it hops along, its diaphragm moves up and down without any muscular effort, emptying and refilling the lungs automatically. The kangaroo's reproductive system is similarly economical. In times of prolonged drought the males become sterile and the female's reproductive system shuts down. In times of plenty, however, it becomes a highly efficient reproduction machine. Females produce up to three staggered offspring at any one time – a young joey hopping around out of the pouch, a smaller joey attached to a nipple in the pouch and a tiny embryo. Females mate within days of giving birth but the new embryo will stop growing when about 25 mm long and remain in a state of suspended animation until its sibling leaves the pouch. This embryonic diapause allows kangaroos to limit their numbers in times of drought and increase them rapidly when food is available.

In cold deserts the problems of aridity are generally less, as they are not exacerbated by evaporation, except through wind. Even so, there is a great range in diversity of adaptation across the three Central Asian deserts.

In the Kyzyl Kum fauna is extremely scarce except for the occasional winter migrant in the northern part of the desert such as the Saiga antelope (*Saiga tatarica*). Animal life in the Taklamakan is less sparse, particularly in peripheral regions of the desert. In river valleys and deltas where water and vegetation appear, there are gazelles and wild boars, wolves and foxes, though tigers, present until the beginning of the twentieth century, are now extinct. Rare animals include the Siberian deer, which inhabits the Tarim River valley, and the wild camel, which at the end of the nineteenth century roamed over much of the Taklamakan but now appears only occasionally in the eastern region. The Gobi Desert, however, sustains a surprising number of animals, including the Bactrian camel, Mongolian wild asses and black-tailed gazelles. In winter, snow leopards, brown bears and wolves are also occasional visitors from the north.

It is fascinating to contrast the adaptations to the aridity of hot deserts with those enabling organisms to survive the intense cold of Antarctica. The best-known and most popular animals of Antarctica are the several species of penguins, stars of the animated film *Happy Feet* (2006) and the feature-length documentary *March of the Penguins* (2005). Penguins have as many strategies to conserve body heat in an ice desert as camels have to cope with hot sand. Interestingly, it is now thought they may have developed one of their most important survival techniques, stabilizing body heat, in a distant evolutionary past when they were still living in warmer climates. They have a network of blood vessels, a plexus, that channels cold blood returning to the body from the flippers and legs past warm blood travelling from the body to these extremities. This counter-current heat exchange warms the cooler blood returning to the body, thus conserving body heat.[21] Emperor penguins (*Aptenodytes forsteri*) also have nasal chambers that can recapture 80 per cent of the heat lost in breathing, while closely aligned veins and arteries enable them to recycle their own body heat.

The internal temperature range of penguins is narrow – from 37.8° to 38.9°c – so maintaining this in water of −2.2°c requires a windproof, waterproof thermal covering. Muscles allow the feathers to be held erect on land, trapping a layer of warmed air next to the skin. Conversely, the plumage is flattened during dives, waterproofing the skin and the downy under-layer. Preening is vital for facilitating insulation and in keeping the plumage oily and water-repellent. The dark plumage of a penguin's dorsal surface absorbs heat from the sun, increasing body temperature. A well-defined fat layer improves insulation in cold water, but is probably not enough to keep body temperature stable at sea for long, so penguins must remain active while in the water to generate sufficient body heat. To conserve heat on land, penguins tuck their flippers in close to their bodies and shiver to generate additional heat. King (*Aptenodytes patagonicus*) and emperor penguins tip their feet up, resting their entire weight on their heels and tail to minimize contact with the icy surface.

The emperor penguin breeds in the coldest conditions on the planet – in air temperatures of −40°c with wind speeds of 144

km per hour – and swims in water of $-2.2°$c. For this it needs supplementary thermal adaptations. Before breeding it develops a layer of sub-dermal fat up to 3 cm thick, which impedes its mobility on land compared to less well-insulated penguins. Its stiff feathers are short, spear-shaped and densely packed over the entire skin surface. With around fifteen feathers per square centimetre, it has the highest feather density of any bird species and an extra layer of insulation is formed by separate shafts of downy filaments between feathers and skin that act like a thermal vest, trapping air. The emperor penguin is able to thermoregulate between $10°$ and $20°$c without altering its metabolism, but below this temperature range its metabolic rate needs to increase significantly. Movement by swimming, walking or shivering are three mechanisms for increasing metabolism; a fourth process involves the raising of blood glucose levels by producing increased levels of the hormone glucagon.

Penguins also have adaptations to reduce their temperature as, on land, overheating may sometimes be a problem. They pant or ruffle their feathers to break up the insulating layer of air next to the skin and release heat. If a penguin is too warm, it holds its flippers away from its body, exposing both surfaces to the air to dissipate heat. A penguin's circulatory system also regulates body temperature. Because they do not 'sweat' but need to expel heat when they walk or just after swimming, blood vessels in the feet of Adélie penguins (*Pygoscelis adeliae*) dilate, making them look pink, but also bringing heat from within the body to the surface, where it is dissipated.

The male emperor penguin incubates its egg for nearly three months, keeping it warm in extreme temperatures under a fold of skin which hangs down over the egg. During this time the male eats nothing, relying on reserves of blubber to keep him alive. In the middle of the Antarctic winter, as many as 6,000 incubating emperor males may huddle together for warmth in what is known as a turtle formation, taking turns to move to the middle where it is warmest – up to $24°$c. This huddling reduces heat loss by up to 50 per cent. By the time the egg hatches, the father will have lost almost half his original body weight, but when the mother returns

Two adult emperor penguins (*Aptenodytes forsteri*) with a juvenile on Snow Hill Island, Antarctica.

from the sea to feed the chick he sets out on the long journey across the ice to replenish his own food supply.

The next chapter will consider the most versatile mammals of all, humans. Our evolution and adaptations have allowed us to endure the extreme living conditions of deserts the world over.

3 Desert Cultures Past and Present

> The Arabs do not speak of desert or wilderness as we do. Why
> should they? To them it is neither desert nor wilderness, but a land
> of which they know every feature, a mother country whose smallest
> product has a use sufficient for their needs. They know, or at least
> they knew in the days when their thoughts shaped themselves
> in deathless verse, how to rejoice in the great spaces and how
> to honour the rush of the storm.
> Gertrude Bell, *The Desert and the Sown* (1907)

In the European imagination deserts are hostile and life-
threatening terrains associated with extreme experiences, treks
through the 'wilderness' and bodily and mental privation: a
challenge to be overcome. Yet archaeological evidence suggests
that from 60,000 years ago humans actively chose to enter desert
lands and remain there, even when they became increasingly
arid.[1] Until the twentieth century human survival in the desert
hinged almost entirely on a nomadic way of life, following seasonal food sources or trading products from the desert for other
necessities at towns or ports. This traditional lifestyle of desert
cultures is now under attack from political and economic forces
as inter-ethnic contact, colonization, industrialization, resource
removal and tourism threaten their way of life, identity and even
their survival.

Bedouin have long been figures of romantic fascination in
the Western imagination. But who actually were the Bedouin
and who are they now? For thousands of years they were warring,
nomadic tribes inhabiting the Arabian Peninsula. They survived
the harsh environment by annual migrations with their herds of
camels, sheep and goats, and gradually spread from the Arabian
Gulf to the Atlantic. Camels, which can travel up to ten days
without water (compared with four days for sheep and two for
cattle), were a family's most precious possessions, providing
milk, meat, hair for tent cloth and clothes, dung for fuel, transport and muscle power for drawing water. They also equipped

Bedouin for surprise attacks and rapid retreats. For centuries Bedouin controlled the desert trade routes, escorting caravans, exacting tolls – like robber barons patrolling the Rhine – and raiding the caravans of other tribes. It has been said that 'the desert is a sea of sand and the Bedouins its roaming pirates.'[2]

Nomadic society was characterized by a fierce loyalty to family, clan and tribe; the tribal chief, the sheikh, elected by the elders, ruled by strength of personality and the protection he offered the tribe. A strict code of behaviour stressed the values of tribal loyalty, female chastity (which included covering the face with a veil or mask), obedience, generosity, hospitality and honour, which involved cycles of revenge killings halted only by blood money as compensation for wrongs. Raiding (*ghazu*), which the early twentieth-century British traveller Gertrude Bell called 'the only industry the desert knows and the only game', boosted a tribe's wealth and preserved a delicate balance of power.[3] Caravans and settled communities alike paid tolls and protection money to avoid raids, which depended for their success on surprise, speed, cunning and guile but rarely involved bloodshed.

Codes of honour emphasized lavish hospitality (*diyafa*) and generosity and any stranger, even an enemy, could be sure of three days' board, lodging and protection. Guests would be served an elaborate meal, even if this meant slaughtering the family's last sheep or borrowing from neighbours.

Most Arabian Bedouin are devout Muslims but because of their precarious existence, they are also by nature fatalistic. Folk superstition is still widespread. Bedouin rarely praise anything directly for fear of the evil eye. Men and animals – and, nowadays, cars and trucks – carry charms or amulets to protect them from evil spirits, or jinn.

Traditional Bedouin nomads lived in long, low, black tents made of goat and camel hair and supported by a line of tall poles in the middle, the number indicating the family's wealth and status. The tent was ideally adapted to desert life: it could be packed up within an hour; it was waterproof, since the wool and hair fabric expanded when wet. It was warm on cold nights and provided shelter from the wind, while in the midday heat the

Syrian Bedouin shepherd photographed while driving his flock of sheep through the ruins to the Palmyra market.

Bedouin women wearing 'falcon' mask burkas, while spinning and knitting, Oman, 1913.

Bedouin family in their tent, Wahiba Sands, Oman, 2005.

sides and back could be rolled up to admit a breeze. The front area of the tent was the men's domain, also used for receiving guests, but the family lived, slept and cooked in the women's quarters behind a dividing curtain. Today wealthy Bedouin families may have an electricity generator installed in their tent for light and power, a television set and other modern appliances, while a tractor and pickup van may be parked outside next to the camels and flocks.

Oases offered an easier lifestyle than the nomadic one and from around the fifth century BCE settlements grew up there, the most important being Mecca. These communities grew dates and grains, becoming small trading centres for caravans transporting spices, ivory and gold from southern Arabia and Africa to the fertile crescent. The hierarchical social distinction between desert nomads, town dwellers and peasant farmers (*fellahin*) is still a characteristic of the Arab world, even though it does not necessarily reflect the relative wealth of these groups.

The vast areas necessary to sustain a nomadic pastoral life are no longer available. Eighteenth-century Ottoman land laws abolished communal ownership of land and, more recently, population expansion, urbanization, industrialization, the oil boom and military demands for bases have severely encroached on traditional rangelands. In the 1950s Saudi Arabia and Syria nationalized Bedouin rangelands, Jordan severely limited goat grazing and Israel reduced the land available to Bedouin in the Negev to force them into villages and towns, the better to control them. Today Bedouin comprise less than 10 per cent of the total Arab population and true nomads less than 1 per cent. Usually the poorest social group, they are marginalized; yet, paradoxically, their traditional nomadic virtues are still held up as the model of pure Arabic-Islamic culture and they are now being urged to enact a traditional lifestyle for the benefit of tourism. Arab governments promote Bedouin theme parks complete with black tents and traditional furnishings and Bedouin dressed as the figures of tourist imagination with the obligatory camels tethered nearby. Arabian Bedouin lifestyle festivals and 'weddings' are immensely popular with visitors,[4] though possibly regarded as degrading by the performers.

The Druze, an esoteric Islamic sect originating in the eleventh century, are found mainly in Syria, Lebanon, Israel and Jordan. Their religion includes elements of Judaism, Christianity, Islam, Gnosticism and Neoplatonism. Rigorous in adhering to principles of honesty, loyalty and filial piety, they were nevertheless militant, suspicious and merciless. Contrasting them with the Bedouin, for whom *ghazu* was a game, Gertrude Bell wrote, 'for [the Druze] it is red war. They do not play the game as it should be played, they go out to slay, and they spare no one . . . they kill every man, woman and child that they encounter.'[5]

Berbers (from the Latin *barbarinus*, 'barbarian'), now numbering some 3 million, are the indigenous people of North Africa west of the Nile Valley. They call themselves Amazigh, meaning 'free people'. Originally a coastal people who practised piracy in the Mediterranean, they were driven south to the Sahara and the Atlas Mountains by successive waves of invaders and colonists, especially by the Arabs, who conquered North Africa in the seventh century.[6] Now racially mixed, the Amazigh are identifiable mainly linguistically as speakers of Tamazight.[7]

Like Bedouin, the Amazigh were traditionally nomads, transporting goods by camel caravan from West Africa and Timbuktu to the Mediterranean. Now most practise agriculture or live in cities in Morocco, Algeria, Tunisia, Libya, Niger and Mali, involved in local crafts such as ironwork, pottery, embroidery and the weaving of kilims, tapestry carpets without a pile.

Having been almost overrun by the Arabs and then the French, the Amazigh have arguably suffered even more since Morocco gained independence from France in 1956. The 65 per cent of Amazigh are the poorest sector of society,[8] and Amazigh activists say that the 'Arabization' of Morocco has led to their state-sanctioned marginalization. Those living outside the cities have no roads, hospitals or running water. Only one in five Amazigh children attends school and there they are taught in Arabic or French. Their history and culture are ignored and parents are required to register their children with Arabic names.[9]

Another threat to Amazigh culture comes from the oil exploration fields near Talsint in southeastern Morocco. To the Amazigh the oil companies are yet another conquering army, paying no compensation to the traditional landowners. The Amazigh have nowhere to go: there is no longer any hinterland where their native culture can survive. But even while they are erasing the Amazigh from the socio-political scene, state authorities exploit them for tourist dollars. Traditionally the Amazigh came in autumn to the rural market at Imilchil in the Atlas Mountains to buy goods for the winter and there young people met and chose partners. Now the annual 'Berber Marriage Festival and Market' is a major tourist event controlled by Arab authorities, who conduct and register mass marriages for a large fee.

The Tuareg are nomadic pastoralists living primarily in Niger, Mali, Algeria and Libya and speaking Berber-related languages. Taking their name from the legendary lost oasis of Targa, they have a little-used but ancient script, Tifinagh.[10] Thought to have descended from Berber nomads, they too became involved in the lucrative trans-Saharan caravan trade, transporting gold, salt, ivory, spices, dates and slaves to Arab traders in the north. In the twentieth century trains and trucks

Tuareg couple with goats, Mali, 1974. The man wears the indigo veil or *tagelmust*, the woman is unveiled.

largely took over the transport system and many Tuareg now live in cities and drive trucks. However, some still carry bars of salt by camel caravan for 600 km on the three-week journey to Timbuktu from the salt mines of Taoudenni in Mali, or from Bilma in Niger.[11] This journey has become a tourist attraction, much photographed from four-wheel drives, but with no financial benefits for the actors. Tuareg are best known for the *tagelmust*, the long indigo-blue veil worn only by the men (hence the name 'Blue Men of the Sahara'). Tightly wound around the head like a turban, covering the whole face except for the eyes, it not only protects against sand and wind but keeps evil jinn from entering through the mouth so that 'the enemy may not know what is in our minds, peace or war'.[12]

Unlike other Muslim cultures, which regard the Tuareg as heretical (*tuareg* is Arabic for 'Abandoned of God'), this society allows women (who do not wear a veil) to play a central role. Social status and political power depend on matrilineal descent and women hold the economic power, owning the family's home and livestock.

Nharo Bushmen (!Kung) drinking water from the bi bulb plant, 2008.

Since North Africa's independence from France the Tuareg have remained a marginalized minority ruled by other racial alliances. During the severe droughts of the 1970s and '80s thousands of Tuareg and their animals died. Niger's exclusion programme deprives them of food relief, medical supplies and development and the Tuareg have scattered deeper into the mountainous Aïr region to escape conflict between militant factions.[13]

Open-strip uranium mining at Arlit, bordering the Aïr Mountains, is a further disaster for the Tuareg, who claim that within two decades their lands will become uninhabitable because of radioactive pollution and aquifer depletion.[14]

The !Kung (where '!' represents the distinctive click consonant characteristic of their language) people live in the Kalahari desert in Namibia, Botswana and Angola, and speak the !Kung language.[15] They are Bushmen, also known as San, Basarwa and Khwe, indigenous people of southern Africa belonging to the Khoisan group (as distinct from the area's majority Bantu population). They are smaller in stature than their Bantu neighbours, with lighter skins and more tightly curled hair, and share with Asian peoples the epicanthal fold, the skin of the eyelid running from the nose to the inner side of the eyebrow. It is now thought that from 25,000 years ago southern and eastern Africa was populated by people closely related to the !Kung and evidence from their unique genetic markers suggests that they are one of the earliest peoples in the world.[16]

The popular film *The Gods Must be Crazy* (dir. Jamie Uys, 1980) rocketed the !Kung to stardom, presenting them as Edenic, gentle and contented hunter-gatherers living in small family groups, sharing what few possessions they had and enjoying their simple lifestyle in a time-forgotten land. This image derived largely from Laurens van der Post's book *The Lost World of the Kalahari* (1958), now discredited as Eurocentric and subjective, and the fieldwork of Harvard ethnographers Richard Lee and Irven DeVore in the 1960s and Lorna and John Marshall in the 1970s. According to these researchers, the !Kung followed a Palaeolithic lifestyle, living in semi-permanent camps of grass-thatched huts surrounding a communal area where family life took place. When water or other resources were depleted, they moved easily to another site, having few possessions to transport. The men hunted using poison-tipped arrows and spears. Arrogance was strongly discouraged, so a successful hunter would share his kill, humbly apologizing for its inadequacy. Women provided most of the food, collecting berries, fruits and nuts, especially the plentiful and nutritious nuts of the Mongongo tree, and ostrich

eggs for water containers.[17] Since there were always adequate
resources for everyone, the anthropologists Marshall Sahlins and
Richard Lee concluded that the !Kung enjoyed 'true affluence',
all their needs being met with about twenty hours of subsistence
work per week, leaving the rest free for leisure, games, singing and
storytelling.[18] This paradisal picture is now largely discounted.
The levels of work were always higher than Lee indicated in the
1960s and inability to store food led to seasonal malnutrition.

Traditionally the !Kung were animists, believing that a spirit
world impacted on them constantly, determining health, sickness, death and food sources. They believed that sickness could
be deflected by a medicine dance or *N/um Tchai* performed by
healers in a self-induced state of trance. This Palaeolithic culture
was long thought to have been overwhelmed in more recent times
by Bantu peoples but in the 1980s and '90s revisionist scholars
asserted that some 2,000 years ago Iron Age, Bantu-speaking
people migrated into !Kung lands, introducing a settled village
lifestyle of herding and cultivation. The !Kung who were in contact with them usually adopted the new way of life, working as
herders, farmers and domestic servants in return for clothing
and protection. Indeed, archaeologists suggest that even before
the Bantu arrived, some !Kung were herding animals rather than
being merely hunter-gatherers.[19]

Modern borehole technology that allows cattle to graze
even in arid lands has finally displaced hunter-gatherers;[20] fences
erected to keep cattle out of tsetse fly areas have disrupted the
migratory routes of wildlife; and because historically they have
had no tribal leaders as spokespersons and no concept of private
ownership, the !Kung have no way to seek redress. Nowadays
their hunting and tracking skills are exploited by farmers to track
poachers and by armies to track guerrillas and map out minefields,
at immense danger to themselves. As 'compensation' governments have forcibly relocated the !Kung to areas with schools
and modern amenities.[21] Daniel Riesenfeld's documentary film
Journey to Nyae Nyae (2006), recording the last weeks of the life
of N!Xau, who played Xi, the lead role in *The Gods Must be Crazy*,
and John Marshall's film *N!ai: The Story of a !Kung Woman*

!Kung families in Namibia.

(1980), present a sad picture of contemporary !Kung. Persuaded to abandon their traditional lifestyle and move to Tjum!kui in return for government handouts, many !Kung now experience crowded living conditions, enforced idleness and major health problems, which have led to alcoholism and family violence.[22]

Today most people have their first encounter with the Australian desert from a plane window as they cross a vast stretch of seemingly featureless country. Yet this land has been home to the world's oldest continuous culture, that of the Australian Aborigines, for more than 50,000 years. So far the earliest human remains found are those of 'Mungo Man', dated at about 40,000 years old,[23] but the time of arrival of the first indigenous Australians is still debated, with estimates ranging back to 125,000 years ago. They are believed to have come from the Indo-Malaysian mainland, via Indonesia and New Guinea, in shallow craft between land bridges exposed during the Pleistocene Ice Ages, when water levels were hundreds of metres below current

heights. It is probable that conditions were more favourable when they first moved south into what is now desert but that in the last Glacial Maximum (some 18,000 years ago) many former water sources and food staples were lost.

Traditional Aborigines were completely self-sufficient. The men hunted large game (bustard, kangaroo, emu and now-extinct megafauna) and the women collected seeds, nuts, fruits, honey ants, at least 92 identified plants and small burrowing animals. Vegetable foods provided between 70 and 80 per cent of their diet, supplemented with goannas, grubs, small mammals and, nowadays, feral cats![24] The ubiquitous spinifex was a multi-purpose resource: it harboured small animals which could be eaten, could be used for starting fires and, when burned slowly, produced a glue-like resin ideal for attaching spear points to shafts. Mulga trees provided shelter, firewood, food, weapons and digging sticks.

An equally essential resource for survival in the desert was underground water, retained in 'soaks' (*mikiri*), shallow aquifers held on underlying stony or clay strata. Reached by long, narrow underground passages which reduce evaporation and spoilage, they require regular cleaning and maintenance to prevent silting up. Ancestral song cycles and dances reminded the tribes of the location of these soaks and of their duty to preserve them. After the arrival of British colonists from 1788 onwards there were inevitable territorial clashes that forced Aborigines from their land and water holes. Deprived of their hunting grounds, they speared sheep for food and the settlers retaliated with guns, often wiping out whole clans. From the 1880s artesian bores became available and settlers and their livestock expanded further into arid areas, radically changing Aboriginal society. Attracted to the missions and settlements by handouts of tea, sugar, flour and tobacco, they were soon enticed to work on pastoral stations, often for little more than their keep until the wage reforms of the 1960s. The hunter-gatherer lifestyle gave way to one in which work was traded for food and clothing.

As important to Aborigines as physical resources is their spiritual identity. This is based on the intimate connection between the Ancestors, the people and animals they created at the time

Aborigine dancer performing at a corroboree in Yulara, Northern Territory, Australia.

of the Dreaming and the land itself – 'country' (these connections will be explained in chapter Five). The spiritual power of
'country' remains immensely strong, even for urban-bred
Aborigines who may never have visited their ancestral land.
But despite this attraction and the many problems they experience in Western society, most Aborigines find the advantages of
a permanent water supply, medical facilities and readily available
food from a shop hard to forego.

The fishermen whom the Spaniards first observed along
the Chilean coast in the sixteenth century were descended from
the Atacameños, the original inhabitants of the Atacama, who
first immigrated to South America some 11,000 years ago.[25]
Middens indicate that for food they drew mainly on the rich
marine resources, catching fish (probably with nets), molluscs, sea
birds, turtles and marine mammals such as sea lions, which they
may have harpooned on the rocky shore. They devised ingenious
tools – thorn or shell fishhooks, bone sinkers, ring-necked nets
and bone harpoon points, as well as stone knives, choppers and
scrapers, fibre cords and reed mats.[26]

There was also seasonal terrestrial food from the desert hinterland when fog from the Pacific created *lomas*, 'small hills' of
vegetation, attracting birds and animals that could be hunted, such
as rodents, foxes and camelids. Fresh water remains scarce: it is
only available in the northern part of the coast by navigating up
the *quebradas* (valleys) to streams from the Andes, and in southern areas in brackish springs.[27] Near the coast, however, water is
now efficiently harvested from fog using vertically mounted mesh
nets with channels beneath them to catch the condensation.[28]

The Atacama remains sparsely populated, with less than
one person per square kilometre. Now largely centred in coastal
cities, fishing villages, oasis communities and inland mining
camps, the indigenous people have been influenced by the ancient
Tiwanaku culture of Bolivia, the Inca and more recently by the
Spanish. In the Altiplano the people herd llamas and alpacas
and grow crops with water from snowmelt streams.

Guano, gathered from the rocky coast, was a lucrative source
of superphosphate and during the nineteenth century the Atacama

Fog collecting nets.

sodium nitrate mines gave Chile a world monopoly on this component of explosives until Germany began to produce synthetic nitrate around 1900. Since the 1950s the Atacama has provided some 30 per cent of the world's copper. However, mines past and present threaten the fragile ecosystems of deserts, as do road construction, grazing by goats and cattle, wood-gathering, increased urbanization and pollution.

Until the early 1800s the Timbisha Shoshone were traditional hunter-gatherers of the Mojave Desert. Although living in small, family-based groups, they were part of a larger cultural/linguistic unit, the Panamint. In winter and spring they lived in the valleys but in summer they migrated to the mountains to collect mesquite pods (*Prosopis glandulosa*) and nuts from the pinyon pine (*Pinus monophylla*). These and other seeds were stoneground into meal and stored for harsher times. Fresh food included tubers, green stalks and the fruit of the endemic Joshua tree. The men hunted bighorn sheep and deer while the women trapped small mammals and gathered plants.

Disruption of this traditional lifestyle began in the 1840s, with mining by the colonists and the processing of gold, silver and borax, which required large quantities of water and

Turkmen man posing with a camel loaded with sacks. The sacks in the background are thought to contain grain or cotton, 1905–15.

wood for furnaces. The pinyon pine and mesquite trees were devastated, depleting game numbers and rendering hunter-gathering unsustainable.

In 1933 Death Valley National Monument was declared a tourist attraction, and ancestral Timbisha land was subsumed by the u.s. federal government, forcing those living within the Monument area to abandon any subsistence activities there. In 1936 the National Park Service constructed a permanent village for them at Furnace Creek and finally, in 1981, the Timbisha Shoshone Tribe was officially recognized by the u.s. government – but without any title to land. They now subsist at Timbisha Village on limited waged work and government assistance, paying the National Park Service for facilities. Because their traditional land now has almost total conservation status, they are not only dispossessed but are unable to pass on their hunter-gathering knowledge and culture. No one under fifty now speaks the Timbisha Shoshone language. The Timbisha Tribe has joined the Western Shoshone National Council, set up to achieve restoration of land rights and native rights and to protest against nuclear activity in the Mojave Desert. Negotiations continue.[29]

From ancient times the people of the Karakum Desert, mainly Turkmen and Uzbeks, were nomadic pastoralists living in demountable yurts around the Caspian Sea and the Amu Darya. They dug deep wells for water and grazed camels, goats and the native karakul sheep, possibly the oldest breed of domesticated sheep, which provided meat, milk, pelts and wool. During the twentieth century the Karakum Canal, running from the Amu Darya, provided extensive irrigation, attracting nearly all the nomadic people to settle on farms, breed livestock on a large scale and grow cotton, fibre crops, fruit and vegetables in oasis areas. Industrialization has brought factories, oil and gas pipelines, railways, roads and powerlines, but the natural resources boom has led to exploitation of sulphur, minerals and building materials and extensive environmental damage.[30]

The Rajasthani people of the Thar desert in northwest India have connections to Indo-Aryan, Indo-Greek and Indo-Iranian ethnic groups and there is linguistic and genetic evidence that Romani people originated in parts of Rajasthan and Gujarat before moving northwest around 1000 CE.[31] Most of the population is engaged in agriculture and animal husbandry, with the result that the land has been overgrazed. This, together with erosion, mining and other industries, has produced severe land degradation and other environmental problems.

Huts in the Thar Desert built with local materials: straw, sand and camel dung.

Indian woman
dressed in an ornate
red sari with traditional
jewellery, in Jaisalmer,
Rajasthan.

Ornaments are important in Rajasthani life. Women wear
elaborate, gem-studded gold and silver ornaments, stitch gold
sequins on their saris and decorate furnishings with silver and
gold ornaments and small pieces of mirror. The Thar is famous
for the vibrant desert Pushkar festivals surrounding the camel fair
held each winter, which attract thousands of tourists. Dressed in
brilliantly coloured costumes, the Rajasthani dance and sing
haunting ballads of courage, romance and tragedy while snake

charmers, puppeteers and acrobats perform and elaborately decorated elephants and camels compete as stars of the festival.

Though it is now so arid, the Gobi Desert has a long history of human habitation. In the past it was notable as part of the great Mongol Empire and for Ürümqi and Dunhuang, important cities along the Silk Road. However, the harsh environment precluded most forms of livelihood and the area remained little known to outsiders, apart from the observations of travellers. By the early twentieth century this region was inhabited mostly by Mongols, Uyghurs and Kazakhs.

The landlocked position, severe climate and rocky geography of the Gobi have preserved a nomadic culture. The main form of shelter is still the traditional *ger* (the Mongolian form of a yurt), the design of which has changed very little over 2,000 years. Heavy felt wrapped around the lattice walls and over the roof provides shelter from the sun during the day and warmth in near-freezing nights.[32] Its light frame can be dismantled or erected in 30 minutes and carried on the back of a camel. The inside is colourfully decorated with embroidered woven hangings and mats and the frame is often carved and painted. Nowadays there are likely to be electrical appliances run from a small generator and motorbikes parked nearby for shopping trips to the nearest towns.

Constructing a *ger* (Mongolian yurt). The wooden lattice frame is being covered with a layer of felt.

In the Tarim Basin in present-day Xinjiang, once an ancient seabed and now occupied by the Taklamakan Desert, mummies up to 4,000 years old have been found. They have been amazingly well preserved by the extreme aridity and salinity of the sand. Chinese archaeologists were astonished to find, in the middle of this extensive desert, mummies buried in upturned boats suggestive of Viking boat burials. Four-metre-high phallic poles rise from the women's boats while the men's boats lie beneath poles to which are attached symbolic vulvas. This veneration of procreation attests to the vital importance of survival in this harsh and isolated environment. Intriguingly, both DNA tests and the physical appearance of these tall, blond or red-haired figures with Caucasoid features, some wearing cloth of tartan design, clearly indicate that these earliest inhabitants of the region were of

Decorated elephant in Jaipur, 2006.

Profile of an Uzbek
woman standing
outside a yurt, dressed
in traditional clothing,
1905–15.

Europoid origin, possibly from the Siberian Steppes and the
borders of Europe.[33] The mummy known as the 'Beauty of Xiaohe'
was an Indo-European woman, who was relatively tall for her
time and had reddish hair; she died in her early forties. Her eyelashes are intact and her teeth show between her parted lips. She
wears a tasselled woollen cloak, fur-lined boots and a stylish felt
hat with a feather.[34] The 'Beauty of Loulan' is also believed to be
of West Eurasian descent, possibly from Siberia or Kazakhstan,
suggesting that the so-called Silk Road had long been a two-way
conduit for plants, animals, technology and ideas.[35] Turkic,
Chinese, Mongol and Tibetan peoples have all left evidence of
their passage. Such controversial findings could affect the claims
of Turkic Uyghurs, 80 per cent of whom live in the Tarim Basin,
to sole indigenous status in the area.

By the early twentieth century the area was under the nom-
inal control of Manchu-China and in 1949 Mao declared it the
Ili Kazakh Autonomous Prefecture, sending Han Chinese to
infiltrate the province to quell dissension. This situation led to
interracial violence in Ürümqi in 2009 and since then many
Chinese settlers have chosen to return to China, leaving the area
to the Uyghurs. However, the Uyghurs remain divided about

The Tarim mummy 'The Beauty of Xiaohe', Tarim Basin, China.

Tarim mummy, 'The Beauty of Loulan', Tarim Basin, China.

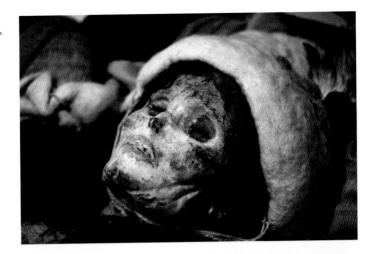

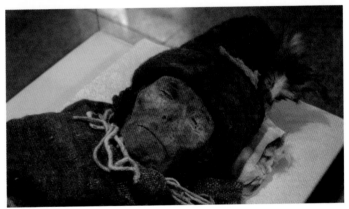

their identity and loyalty, unsure whether to align themselves on religious grounds, supporting a pan-Islamic vision, or according to racial grounds, as a pan-Turkic organization, or to support formation of an independent state of Uyghurstan.

In the next chapter the artistic expressions of ancient desert cultures will be explored. From the mimetic rock art of Africa to the semiotic designs and ephemeral ground paintings of the Australian Aborigines, this prehistoric art raises a host of intriguing and politically controversial speculations about its aesthetic sophistication, its spiritual context, and the climatic changes it depicts.

Camel and owner rest during a desert crossing in Sam, Rajasthan, India.

87

4 Museums of Our Ancestors

The motivation of these ancient artists is lost in time, but although
we do not have the key to interpret the most ancient art of this
continent [Australia], an enormous body of designs engraved
on rocks and painted on caves of more recent origin provides
a fascinating visual record of the history of man and the unique
culture which evolved on this continent.
Jennifer Isaacs, *Australian Dreaming* (1980)

The arts and crafts of nomadic and hunter-gatherer cultures are
necessarily either portable, like the beautifully decorated yurts of
the Central Asian deserts; ephemeral, like the ground and body
paintings of the Australian Aborigines; or, like rock engravings or
paintings, left behind when a community departs.

In its most ancient forms, rock art comes to us from forebears
so remote as to be common ancestors to all mankind, reminding
us of what we share as human beings. It may suggest a different
purpose for artistic expression: whereas Western art focusses on
the aesthetic, it appears that rock art was intended in most cases
to convey a transforming spiritual experience.

Like the earliest humans, the earliest known example of art
comes from Africa. A piece of ochre estimated to be 77,000 years
old and decorated with a delicate geometric pattern was found
at Blombos Cave in the Southern Cape of South Africa, along
with red and yellow ochre pigments mixed in abalone shells and
tools for extracting and mixing these pigments.[1] This ancient 'art
studio' has been dated at 100,000 years old, while fragments of
painted stone discovered at the Apollo 11 rock shelter in Namibia
are believed to be at least 19,000 years old, possibly 26,000 years.

In the time of the pharaohs, people were painting on rock
surfaces in the centre of the Sahara, but they were painting over
other art that was already 6,000 years old. More than 3,000 sites
have now been found in the Sahara where engravings, or petroglyphs, were painstakingly pecked or incised into rocks and images

were painted on rock surfaces. Most of the earliest engravings found in the central Saharan mountains, dating from about 10,000 years ago and showing large wild animals, are 20–100 cm tall, though some are up to 5 m high. At Tassili n'Ajjer and the Acacus and Ennedi Mountains, paintings dated between 8000 and 6000 BCE show humans, mainly in profile, some wild animals and, later, domesticated cattle. These were first discovered in 1933 by a patrol policeman, Lieutenant Brenans, who was riding into Wadi Oued Djerat on the Tassili n'Ajjer massif. He was astonished to see, engraved on the rock walls of this desolate, 'lunar' landscape, the most remarkable collection of prehistoric engravings in the Sahara. More than 15,000 drawings and engravings have now been found on the Tassili n'Ajjer plateau on the borders of Algeria and Libya,[2] recording climatic changes, animal migrations and the history of human life from 8000 to 1900 BCE. The earliest paintings show a well-watered savannah with water-loving animals – rhinoceroses, giraffes, elephants, buffalos, hippopotamuses and crocodiles – and people swimming or in boats on a river. Those

Petroglyph depicting a possibly sleeping antelope at Tin Taghirt on the Tassili n'Ajjer in southern Algeria.

painted more recently than 2,000 years ago show the Sahara as a desert. The French explorer and ethnographer Henri Lhote, who visited Tassili n'Ajjer in 1939, distinguished five periods in Saharan rock art, depicting animals that indicate the climate change from wet savannah to grazing and hunting lands to desert.

Rock paintings and engravings have now been discovered at many sites in the Sahara. Wadi Mathendous in southwest Libya, for example, has large petroglyphs of animals including elephants, giraffes, hippos, meerkats and aurochs (large, extinct wild cattle).

In the dry, mountainous Gilf Kebir region in southwest Egypt is the Cave of the Swimmers, discovered in 1933 by the Hungarian explorer László Almásy in the base of Wadi Sura, where a river once flowed. In this sandstone cave are paintings of animals, including giraffes, ostriches and long-horned cows, and diminutive people, who are unmistakably swimming and diving. The paintings are estimated to date from 8,000 to 10,000 years ago, when the region was clearly well-watered. A painted set of the cave, created for Anthony Minghella's 1996 film of Michael Ondaatje's novel *The English Patient* (1992), set a fashion for tours to visit the actual cave, leading, sadly, to extensive damage to the paintings.

Henri Lhote with rock art in the Sahara Desert of Mauritania, 1967.

Rock carving of elephant in Tadrart Acacus, Libya, reflecting the dramatic climate change in this area.

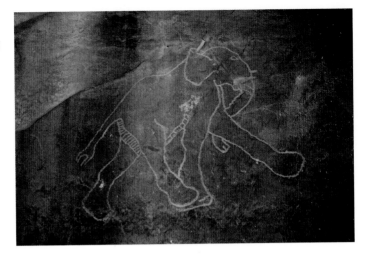

Further south, in the Kalahari, the Tsodilo Hills in northwest Botswana contain one of the most concentrated collections of rock art in the world, more than 4,500 paintings within an area of 10 square km, most executed by the !Kung. Some are dated to 24,000 years ago. Many of the red paintings feature geometric symbols, human figures and animals with disproportionate body parts. Pictures with cattle date from 600 to 1200 CE, following their introduction after the sixth century CE. Whereas Saharan rock art ceased to be created some 2,000 years ago, the !Kung were still producing rock paintings in the nineteenth century, when anthropologists could interrogate artists or their contemporaries and when people who had seen the paintings executed were still alive. Some of these paintings depict people riding horses, which arrived there only in the 1850s.

Early observers of !Kung rock art interpreted it as being naturalistic representations of animals, intended to secure a good outcome in the hunt. More recently, and particularly as a result of the revisionist work of David Lewis-Williams, the figures, both human and animal, are now understood to represent the spiritual experiences and altered states of consciousness of shamans. Lewis-Williams and Thomas Dowson have suggested that the spirit world was believed to exist behind the rock wall and that the images were seen by the !Kung as emerging through the rock 'veil'.[3]

The eland, the largest of the African antelopes, is the most frequently painted animal here and Lewis-Williams noted that artists concentrated in particular on the distinctive stance and characteristics of the *dying* eland, with lowered head, hollow, staring eyes, erect hair, sweat pouring from the body, crossed hind legs and blood gushing from the nostrils. In painting after painting these features are recorded with the same care with which Christian artists depicted the details of the Crucifixion.

In one particular painting portraying a dying eland and a man apparently holding its tail, Lewis-Williams observed that the man displayed the same distinguishing features as the animal. He developed a theory that the !Kung revered and depicted the eland not just as a food source but as a source of spiritual power, which enabled shamans to 'become' a therianthrope of the eland. Empowered by the eland's spirit, the shaman could cure the sick, lead animals to hunters or induce rain. Thus this art celebrating the dying eland and the transference of its powers preserved both the awareness of the animal's importance and reverence for the shamans' power.

Hunting scene, Tassili n'Ajjer.

A strongly spiritual element is also integral to Australian Aboriginal art, which expresses an abundance of life and sacred meaning in the desert landscape. Australian Aboriginal art is unique among indigenous art in that it is still evolving in many styles and media and captivating an international market.

The oldest known Australian rock paintings, the Bradshaw figures, are also the most intriguing, and the most politically controversial. Located in northwestern Australia in the remote and rugged area of the Kimberley, the examples already documented form the largest concentration of Upper Paleolithic Ice Age rock art in the world, and it is estimated that there may be many more – up to 100,000 galleries of paintings.[4] They are named after Joseph and Frederick Bradshaw, pastoralists who, in 1891, found caves 'adorned with native drawings coloured in red, black, brown, yellow, white and a pale blue'.[5] Joseph immediately noted the 'attenuated' bodies of the figures, their 'tassel-shaped adornments', their aquiline features, their similarity to those of ancient Egyptian art and their apparent age. Between the 1930s and '60s anthropologists commented on the artistic sophistication and sense of movement of these delicate figures, their unusual attire and their great age – far older than the *Wandjina* figures in the same area. Local Aborigines dissociated themselves from the Bradshaws, insisting that the figures were made by a

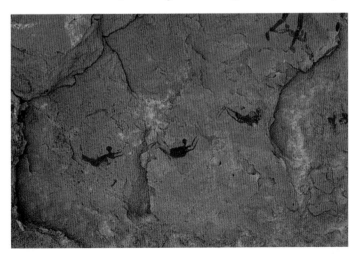

Swimming figures in the Cave of Swimmers, Gilf Kebir plateau, Libyan Sahara.

bird (called *gwion gwion*), which pecked out the outline and painted the characteristic red colour of many of the figures with its own blood.[6] In the 1970s a park ranger named Grahame Walsh became so fascinated with the figures that he devoted the rest of his life to recording them, leaving an archive of 1.2 million transparencies, stills, sketches and detailed analyses of the figures and the brush strokes.[7]

Walsh categorized the Bradshaws according to their distinctive clothing. 'Tassel' Bradshaws, typically 200–800 mm high,

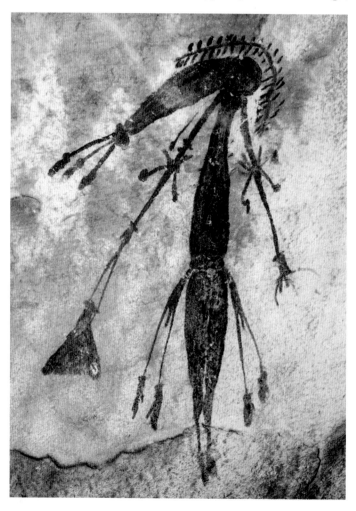

Tassel Bradshaw figure with 'fan' and 'tram-track' headdress, Kimberley, Western Australia.

From a panel showing a dying eland with a therianthrope holding the tail of the eland. Game Pass Shelter, Kamberg, Natal Drakensberg, Africa. The therianthrope's legs are crossed in imitation of the eland's crossed hind legs and terminate under the rock ledge in carefully drawn black antelope hoofs.

display tassels attached to a wide waistband, ankles, elbows, arms and chest, and elaborate, elongated headdresses which either hang over one shoulder or extend backwards or upwards. 'Sash' Bradshaws, of a similar size, wear a wide, three-pointed waist sash and even more exaggerated headdresses, some with a pair of wings on top.[8] Experts invited to date some of the Bradshaws using different methods obtained figures varying from 4,000 to 21,000 years old, but 6,000 years is a conservative estimate.[9]

Walsh claimed that the Bradshaws were unique, superior to any other Aboriginal art in style, composition, aesthetic standard and technique, and in the freshness, vitality, elegance and sophistication of the dancing figures.[10] He proposed that the Bradshaw artists were a distinct ethnic group who had arrived in Australia long before Aboriginal peoples and then either departed, or been overcome by the later wave or waves of migration. This suggestion is vehemently opposed by those who claim that Aborigines were the original inhabitants of the continent, but numerous Aboriginal stories exist about a smaller, darker race of artistically advanced people in ancient times.[11] Recent research on the

95

similarities between species of African baobab trees (*Adansonia digitata*) and the boab tree of the Kimberley (*A. gregorii*) suggests that the latter may have been transported to the Western Australian coast some 60–70,000 years ago, possibly by the people who produced the Bradshaw rock art. There are images of boab fruit and flowers in the art, and large boats with high prows, capable of carrying up to 30 people appear in the paintings. Most tellingly, the Bradshaw art is more reminiscent of contemporary African art than of any other.[12]

Traditional Aboriginal art forms varied greatly across the continent, but they always had a spiritual purpose, a reflection of universal order laid down by the Ancestors. Ground mosaics, sometimes extending over 100 square m, are the most spectacular and ephemeral art form of the desert regions. Chopped leaves, stems and flowers are rolled into pellets with animal fat and dyed with red or yellow ochre, white clay or black charcoal. These are laid on the ground to create a geometric design. In the centre is a hole into which a pole of phallic significance may be placed. The mosaic is intimately linked to the performance of sacred rituals in song and dance, which 'open' the land and induce the creative power of the Ancestors to emerge and enter into the male dancers, whose bodies are painted in elaborate designs, with feathers and down stuck on with animal fat. As they dance, the down floats from their bodies to the ground, symbolizing semen and fertility being returned to the earth. The brilliance of the white down against black skin also symbolizes the Ancestors' sacred energy. Thus dancers, artists and singers together recreate the land. In the process the ground mosaics are inevitably destroyed, but their brightly coloured pellets inspired the famous dot paintings of the Western Desert.

Unique to the Kimberley region in northwestern Australia are the striking *Wandjina* figures painted on the walls of caves and dating from about 1,500 years ago. Up to 7 m tall, these human-looking figures have round heads emphasized by a 'halo' of radiating lines indicating the lightning of the wet season. Their simplified faces have large, arresting and heavily lashed black eyes, often joined to a beak-like nose, but no mouths. If

Detail from a painting
of a ground design by
an Aborigine of
Papunya, 1971.

Pintupi men preparing for a ceremony involving body painting, Western Desert, Australia, 1984.

they had these, it is believed, water would pour forth from them, flooding the land.[13] Usually painted on a white background, their facial features are outlined in red ochre with occasional black and yellow markings, so they appear to leap out from the dark walls of the cave. *Wandjina* were central to a religious cult, *wunan*, connected to the fertility of the land, the seasons and the conception of children.[14] Aborigines of the area believe that these figures are actual embodiments of the Ancestral *Wandjina*, who lay down in caves and 'became' the paintings. Thus no new images can be made, though the existing ones must be retouched to ensure rain. Because most Aboriginal art remains associated with a living, spiritual tradition, it is a ritual obligation for guardians of the Law of the Ancestors, the *Tjukurpa*, to retouch fading rock art images,[15] a practice that often distresses non-Aboriginal purists who wish to preserve them intact.

Whereas the *Wandjina* are static figures, the 'dynamic style' *Mimi* figures painted on the rocks of West Arnhem Land and Kakadu are stick-like, indicating that they are thin spirits able to pass through cracks in the rock. They are believed to have taught the people how to paint the x-ray images of animals characteristic of West Arnhem Land during the last 3,000 years. In this striking technique, outlines of animals are infilled with complex geometric patterns and fine cross-hatched designs to indicate their internal structure and organs. Fatty deposits are often presented in yellow as a guide to this scarce, nutritious component of their diet.

These many styles of traditional art continue to inspire contemporary artists who use modern media, such as acrylic paints on canvas or boards, or batik designs on fabric. Traditionally, only those associated by birth and ritual initiation with a particular area had the authority to paint the map of their country. This has now been accepted in Australian law and art depicting country has played an important part in the struggle of Aboriginal people to regain their land rights.[16]

The Chinchorro people, who occupied a 650-km stretch of the western coast of South America, produced the oldest known religious objects in their intriguing and elaborate mummies dating from 5050 BCE, millennia before their Egyptian counterparts. These mummies have survived because of the extreme hyper-aridity of the Atacama Desert. Their production was a complex, intricate process. First the skin was carefully removed and set aside, and the skeleton reinforced with sticks. The organs were replaced with clay ones and the flesh with bundles of reeds and sea grass before the skin was put on again, patched, where necessary, with sea lion skin. The whole body was then covered with ash paste and

Wandjina figures, Kimberley, Western Australia.

painted with black manganese dioxide. Clay masks with carefully modelled facial features and small slits for eyes and mouth to give the impression of a sleeping person, and wigs of human hair were added. The finished products gleamed like polished statues. Unlike Egyptian mummies that were buried in tombs, they appear to have been cared for and revered by the relatives of the deceased within their homes, perhaps to ease the passage to the afterlife, or to induce them to lobby the gods for family favours.

Around 2500 BCE the manganese supply may have become exhausted, because the black mummies were replaced by mummies coated with red ochre. These were produced more simply, without removing the skin. Organs and muscles were replaced with clay, reeds and llama fleece before the mummies were plastered with ochre. The red mummies have open eyes and mouths, suggesting wakefulness rather than sleep, and an entry point for the soul wishing to reinhabit its body. Both red and black mummies were probably displayed in shrines or used in processions,[17] as was the Inca practice at the time of Spanish colonization, and

Rock painting of *Mimi* figures in the Anbangbang Gallery at Nourlangie Rock, Arnhem Land, Kakadu National Park, Northern Territory.

as statues of the Virgin or Hindu deities are carried in religious processions today, both to honour them and to petition for favours. Whereas the Egyptians accorded elaborate mummification and burial only to royal family members, the Chinchorro honoured all social classes and ages, including young children and infants, but by 2000 BCE prepared mummies had given way to bodies that were desiccated naturally in the dry atmosphere, then buried under a layer of mud.

Dunhuang, an oasis town in the bleak desert region of China, occupied a strategic position on the Silk Road and, as indicated by the Tarim mummies, was a nexus between European and Asian civilizations for more than 2,000 years. It was particularly influenced by the spread of Buddhist beliefs and art from India. Between the fourth and the fourteenth centuries, Buddhist monks oversaw the construction of a series of stone-cut cave temples for meditation, devotion and the translation of sutras, a practice that had begun in ancient India and spread along the Silk Road.

At Mogao, about 25 km southeast of Dunhuang, a complex of caves was cut into a cliff beside the Daquan River, and decorated with hundreds of spectacular Buddhist murals painted across the arched ceilings and walls. According to legend, a Buddhist

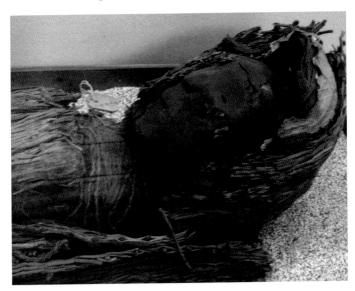

Head of a mummy from the Chinchorro culture, found in northern Chile and dating from *c*. 3000 BCE.

Ancient Buddhist painting on silk, showing Vaiśravana, demon-king of the northern realm, moving with divine host across the ocean. Discovered at the Mogao Caves (Caves of the Thousand Buddhas), Dunhuang, Gansu, China.

monk, Yuezun, had a vision in 366 CE of 1,000 Buddhas and he, with other wandering monks, carved out caves until, after a millennium, there were over 1,000. About 500 were decorated as temple caves, with murals, statues and architecture serving as aids to meditation and acting as teaching tools to inform illiterate Chinese people about Buddhist beliefs and stories. During the long period of construction there were invasions, migrations and changes of ruler, each successive wave adding its own traditional art, culture and scenes from daily life. In some caves a large Buddha is surrounded by Indian, European or Persian figures, as well as by Uyghur princes and princesses, monks and travellers.

Most of the art has a clear Buddhist focus, depicting stories of sutras against a background of scenery or buildings. Bodhisattvas are depicted as Indian princes, and Apsaras (female celestial beings) abound, but other beliefs are also recorded: Confucianism, Daoism, Manichaeism, Zoroastrianism and Nestorianism. There are also intriguing depictions of daily life, showing people of different races and skin colours participating in rituals or making music together. The cave images suggest a multicultural interconnectedness and racial and religious tolerance rarely seen today. Some murals are artistically naive but others are highly sophisticated religious art, and in 1987 the Mogao Caves complex was declared a UNESCO World Heritage site, known as the Caves of the Thousand Buddhas.[18]

When a maritime alternative to the Silk Road was developed, the dangerous and difficult land routes were abandoned and the oasis towns were largely forgotten. The few monks remaining at the caves were unaware that a vast collection of scriptures from the West had been sealed up in Cave 17, the so-called Library Cave,

Ming dynasty mural of bodhisattvas found at the Mogao Caves in Dunhuang, now at Fahai Temple in Beijing.

behind a wall painting. This treasure, the archaeological find of the twentieth century, was discovered in 1900 by a Taoist monk, Wang Yuanlu, self-appointed abbot and guardian of the caves. In 1907 Marc Aurel Stein, a British-Hungarian archaeologist and explorer who had heard rumours about the treasure, arrived in Mogao and persuaded Wang Yuanlu to show him the interior. He wrote:

> Heaped up in layers but without any order, there appeared in the dim light of the priest's little lamp a solid mass of manuscript bundles rising to a height of nearly ten feet . . . hidden behind a brick wall . . . these masses of manuscripts had lain undisturbed for centuries.[19]

Earliest known illustration of a fire lance and a grenade, Dunhuang, 10th century. Illustration of Shakyamuni's (Buddha's) temptation by Mara, with demons at the upper right threatening with the fire lance, grenade and other weapons, while those at lower right tempt with pleasures.

Stein found up to 50,000 manuscripts, hundreds of paintings on silk and paper, sutras, textiles and other artefacts, amassed over centuries, together with priceless Buddhist texts written in Sanskrit, Sogdian, Tibetan, Runic-Turkic, Chinese, Uyghur and other languages that Stein could not identify. From the Dunhuang paintings, Stein realized that 'the influence of Graeco-Buddhist models [had] victoriously spread itself to the Far East'. He named this new style of art, which depicted the Buddha in human form, Serindian.[20] Hellenistic influences were apparent in the Buddha's drapery, in figures wearing Phrygian caps, a four-horse Roman chariot and an inscription indicating the artist's name as a derivative of the Roman name Titus.[21] As well as the floating drapery of the Chinese style, he noted the dignified, serene features, the simple yet impressive gestures and the graceful folds of clothing characteristic of classical art.[22]

Stein's most valuable discovery was the Diamond Sutra, printed in the ninth year of the Xiantong Era of the Tang Dynasty (that is, 868 CE), approximately 587 years before the first Gutenberg Bible and the earliest complete example of a dated, printed book. In the manner of a Socratic dialogue, it concerns the Buddha's attempt to help a man, Subhuti, to question his preconceptions about the nature of reality and enlightenment. It concludes with an image that recalls Plato's famous analogy of the prisoners in the

A page from the Diamond Sutra, printed in the 9th year of the Xiantong Era of the Tang dynasty (868 CE), the earliest complete survival of a dated printed book.

Ancient embroidery on silk, showing Buddha between disciples and bodhisattvas, with the donors in adoration below. Discovered at the Mogao Caves, Dunhuang.

cave: 'All conditioned phenomena / Are like dreams, illusions, bubbles or shadows . . .'.[23]

Stein persuaded Wang Yuanlu to sell him 7,000 complete manuscripts, 6,000 fragments and cases of paintings, embroideries and other artefacts for £220; the money was to be used for the restoration of the other caves. This treasure horde of manuscripts is now in the British Museum in London, and the paintings have been divided between the National Museum in New Delhi and the British Museum.[24] Stein was soon followed by other collectors, who also removed manuscripts, statues and even slabs of wall containing murals. Visiting journalists and photographers gave the world a detailed account of the treasures, leading to the establishment of the Dunhuang Institute for Cultural Relics in 1951 and the listing of the Mogao Caves as a Cultural Treasure of National Importance by the Chinese government in 1961.[25]

Most of the traditional art discussed in this chapter had a religious purpose, even if that purpose is now unclear to us. But deserts have also inspired religions that left few or no pictorial records: the major monotheistic religions. These, together with the spirit beliefs of the Australian Aborigines and more recent secular cults of the desert, will be considered in the next chapter.

5 Desert Religions

> The great concepts of oneness and of majestic order seem always
> to be born in the desert.
> John Steinbeck, *Travels with Charley* (1962)

When we think of the world's great religions, we are likely to
envisage vast numbers of people crowding into cathedrals, syna-
gogues, mosques or St Peter's Square, circling the Kaaba in
Mecca or attending mass evangelist rallies. Yet the three great
monotheistic world faiths, Judaism, Christianity and Islam,
originated in the deserts of the Middle East, among people of
few material possessions and little political power. The desert
has continued to hold an important place in the ideology of
these religions, even as they have spread across the world, becoming increasingly urbanized and associated with wealth, power
and impressive architecture. The Greek word *eremos*, root of the
English 'hermit', means desert; and solitude, as epitomized in
retirement to desert places, has continued to attract philosophers
and religious devotees to this day. The Old Testament prophets
and the Desert Fathers and Mothers of early Christianity, who
sought spiritual enlightenment away from earthly temptations,
became the inspiration for medieval monasticism, with its emphasis on abstinence, poverty and rigour, and for the focus on
spiritual self-examination that was characteristic of nineteenth-
century Evangelical pietism. This chapter traces the continuing
connections between the minimal materialism of desert life
and the pursuit of monotheistic spiritual practices, as well as the
beliefs of some indigenous desert peoples and the appeal they
exert on the West.

From earliest times, the desert, the biblical 'wilderness', has
been an ambiguous concept in Judaeo-Christian theology. On the

Thomas Cole, *Expulsion from the Garden of Eden*, 1828, oil on canvas.

one hand it was a perpetual reminder of the Fall, the disobedience of Adam and Eve and their expulsion from the Garden of Eden into the desert wilderness (Genesis 3:17–19), and a continuing warning that disobedience to God would perpetuate the curse laid upon Adam: 'The Lord shall make the rain of thy land powder and dust' (Deuteronomy 28:23–4). Thus, in contrast to the Edenic garden, the desert signified a dreaded place, a place of sin, where survival is doubtful. On Yom Kippur, the Day of Atonement, the Jewish high priest symbolically laid the sins of the people on the head of a goat, a 'scapegoat', which was then driven into the wilderness, bearing their sins away, as prescribed in Leviticus (16:8, 10, 26).

Yet the desert also came to be seen as a place of spiritual purification and enlightenment by virtue of both its physical harshness, which generated dependence on divine blessing, and its lack of material and sensory distractions from spiritual contemplation. Thus, for the pilgrim seeking spiritual enlightenment by transcending his or her earthly surroundings through bodily discomfort, the otherwise inimical aspects of the desert become virtues. Absence of material comforts promotes concentration on the divine; physical hardships produce spiritual athletes; the vast, isolated expanse without sensory stimulation presents a training course for the soul, testing the individual's ability to stand alone before God.

As an alternative to divine revelation, other explanations have been proposed for the desert origins of monotheistic religions. A desert landscape under a vast, monochromatic sky may suggest a unified world, the work of one creator, whereas a scene in which the eye is continually diverted by trees, rivers or mountains encourages either an animistic view that individual objects have an independent existence created by separate spirit beings, or a rationalist paradigm of the world as a collection of material objects under our control.

Historically, Christianity and Islam share a common stem in Judaism, which originated as the religion of a group of Semitic nomads in the Arabian Desert.[1] The Hebrews (*Ibri*) were one of hundreds of Semitic tribes that settled in Mesopotamia, 'The Land Between Two Rivers' (modern-day Iraq and parts of Syria, Turkey and Iran), after migrating from the Arabian Peninsula. In the early part of their history these herdsmen had neither the resources to build temples nor, perhaps, the artisanal skills to craft idols. Essentially they needed a deity that would accompany them, symbolized in the pillar of cloud by day and the pillar of fire by night that guided the Israelites in their journey from Egypt towards Canaan, as described in Exodus (13:21–2). Both these effects may have emanated from the then-active volcano Mt Sinai (not the present-day Mt Sinai but Mt Hor in Arabia).[2]

In *The Seven Pillars of Wisdom*, written out of his experience of living for many years with Arabs, T. E. Lawrence characterized Semitic peoples as being moulded by the desert and its traditions. Many of the qualities he ascribed to them can be seen as contributing to their religious beliefs and practices. He described them as dogmatic, fatalistic and impervious to argument, with clear, hard beliefs, and as despising doubt.

Their thoughts were at ease only in extremes. They inhabited
superlatives by choice . . . Their creeds were assertions, not
arguments; so they required a prophet to set them forth . . .
None of them [the prophets] had been of the wilderness;
but . . . [an] unintelligible passionate yearning drove them
out into the desert. There they lived a greater or lesser time
in meditation and physical abandonment; and thence they
returned with their imagined message articulate . . . [But]
this faith of the desert was impossible in the towns. It was at
once too strange, too simple, too impalpable for export and
common use.[3]

Judaism, the oldest continuing monotheistic religion, began
among a Semitic tribe that migrated from the Arabian Desert
to the Fertile Crescent.[4] As successive waves of nomadic people
arrived to enjoy this fruitful land, there were continued tribal
wars between the sedentary inhabitants and the dispossessing
invaders, each of whom were armed with their traditional gods.
The patriarchal figure Abram (later Abraham), a nomadic leader
from about 1,800 BCE from whom all Jews claim descent, came
from Ur of the Chaldees to settle in Canaan (roughly corresponding to modern Israel). His significance in Judaism arises from his
covenant with his God, YHWH (or Yahweh), according to which
his descendants, the 'Chosen People', would receive divine protection in return for fulfilling God's laws. A severe drought in
Canaan caused Abraham's grandson Jacob and his sons to migrate
to Goshen in northern Egypt. There, according to the Hebrew
Bible, Jacob's descendants were at first welcomed but later enslaved,
escaping only through divine intervention. This exodus was
thenceforth celebrated as a focal point of Judaism, evidence of
the Jews' status as the Chosen People.

According to the Torah, the Israelites, led by the prophet
Moses, spent 40 years traversing the Sinai Desert before reaching Canaan, the Promised Land. During this time they received
from Yahweh the Ten Commandments at Mt Sinai, reinforcing
their unique identity and distinguishing them from other desert
tribes that did not observe these rules. Chief amongst these was

the requirement to worship only one God, Yahweh. This period in the desert wilderness was integral to generating their sense of unity as a nation and imprinting the need for reliance on a God, who was a 'combination of mountain spirit, storm and volcanic deity, and wilderness guide'.[5] The later story of Elijah being fed by ravens in the desert (1 Kings 17) recalled the Israelites' dependence on manna, the divinely provided food that sustained them throughout their journey through the wilderness (Exodus 16:14–24). Thus although the desert was a dreaded place beset with constant dangers from other tribes, it was also associated with divine protection, guidance and sustenance. These pastoral nomads had little or no private property or material luxuries such as they acquired once they settled in Canaan. When the nation became rich, materialistic and forgetful of God, it was two men of the wilderness or semi-wilderness community – Elijah in the ninth century BCE and Amos in the eighth century BCE – who protested in the name of Yahweh against the moral corruption of Israel (1 Kings 1 and Amos 1:1). Gertrude Bell, a British traveller in the early twentieth century, wrote of the desolation of this Israeli desert and its prophetic power:

> And yet the Wilderness of Judaea has been nurse to the fiery spirit of man. Out of it strode grim prophets, menacing with doom a world of which they had neither part nor under-standing; the valleys are full of the caves that held them, nay, some are peopled to this day by a race of starved and gaunt ascetics clinging to a tradition of piety that common sense has found it hard to discredit.[6]

The Hebrew Bible prophets not only came from the wilderness; they periodically returned there to reset their spiritual compasses before confronting resistant rulers and erring people. Sojourn in the desert became almost an obligatory prerequisite for prophecy, just as fasting and prayer were symbolic reminders of the Israelites' time in the wilderness.

In the second century BCE a group of Jews known as the Essenes chose to move from Jerusalem into the desert, possibly

Caves at Qumran in the
West Bank, Middle
East, where the Dead
Sea Scrolls were found.

to Qumran, to pursue a life of asceticism, voluntary poverty, extreme
cleanliness, strict dietary rules and abstinence from worldly pleasures. John the Baptist was almost certainly an Essene and it has
been suggested that Jesus, too, came from this group; but, if so,
he departed from their strict regimen of fasting and obligatory
ritual washing.[7]

Yet with the exception of minority groups like the Essenes
and the Pharisees, Judaism has never embraced asceticism, or

even abstinence, beyond the five prescribed days of fasting.[8] Throughout most of the Old Testament, wealth and material goods were interpreted as signs of God's approval and blessing and in modern Jewish teaching wealth is respected as the necessary means to provide a good Jewish home, education for children and generosity to the community and the poor. Some notable Jewish rabbis have even denounced asceticism as a sin.[9] The significance of this desert heritage has been largely submerged, except in the ritual Feast of the Tabernacles (Sukkot), when families commemorate the 40 years in the wilderness after the Exodus by erecting small 'booths' (sukkah) with walls of plaited branches and a roof (sekhakh) made of organic material that has grown in the ground, such as branches, stalks or reeds, and through which the sky can be seen.[10]

In theory at least, a more lasting embrace of what we might call desert values has been retained in Christianity, where self-denial, simplicity and poverty have been repeatedly, if intermittently, affirmed as desirable spiritual attributes. Jesus and his disciples were raised as Jews, and early Christianity grew out of Jewish belief, particularly in regard to monotheism and the moral message of the prophets. It was recorded that before beginning his ministry, Jesus was 'led up of the Spirit into the wilderness' and fasted for 40 days and nights alone in the desert, a reference to the time Moses and Elijah spent fasting in the wilderness. Physically weak but spiritually strengthened, he withstood the temptations to miraculously provide bread to satisfy his hunger, to perform spectacular feats and to claim earthly power and prestige, all of which run counter to the desert-derived emphasis on abstinence and a simple lifestyle (Matthew 4:1–11; Mark 1:12–13; Luke 4:1–13).

Christians of the first century CE had little time for the privation and voluntary self-denial of the wilderness experience. Often in peril of persecution and execution, they concentrated on founding churches in the urban centres of the Roman Empire rather than cultivating desert retreats. However, after 313 CE, when Emperor Constantine I legalized Christianity, there was no physical danger in being a Christian; only the spiritual danger of becoming comfortable. Although the crown of martyrdom was no longer readily available, there remained the possibility of seeking spiritual purification in the wilderness. It was in this climate that St Anthony of Egypt founded a retreat at Dayr al-Maymun in 270–71 CE, initiating a movement of Christian ascetics to the desert to form communities of solitude, austerity and sacrifice. Self-denial, especially sexual abstinence, fasting and prayer, were the treasures offered by the desert experience. St Jerome allegedly declared, 'To me a town is a prison, and the desert loneliness a paradise.'[11] Indeed, in Egypt and Syria during the first century CE, desert monasticism became so popular with Desert Fathers and Desert Mothers and those who flocked to consult them that, to the distress of the original retreatants, the desert became virtually 'a city'.[12] Yi-Fu Tuan suggests that there was 'more than a touch of misanthropy among the desert hermits and the early Church Fathers who sought solitude for themselves'.[13] They resented humanity as a distraction from the overwhelming vastness that facilitated contemplation of the eternal.

In this context the notion of 'desert' was often interpreted as perceptual rather than geographical, involving voluntary exile from a nearby town rather than extreme physical isolation. This can be seen in Giovanni Bellini's painting *St Jerome in the Desert*, with the elegant Italianate towers of a nearby town prominent in the composition.

The religious significance of the desert was its ability to generate contemplation of the numinous, awe of the divine. In his seminal work, *The Idea of the Holy* (1917), the German Lutheran theologian Rudolf Otto defined the numinous as a mystery that is both terrifying and fascinating.[14] Three of the predominant responses to desert – awe at its immensity, terror at its starkness and fascination at its wildness – parallel these characteristics of *mysterium*, *tremendum* and *fascinans*. Vacant distance – infinity in the horizontal plane – represents the Sublime transposed to the spatial. Such overwhelming extension in space evokes a corresponding sense of infinity in time – eternity – and many find the experience of this spatial-temporal combination intense, vision-producing, almost literally mind-blowing, since it transcends the rational.

Inside the grounds of St Anthony's Monastery at Coma, Egypt.

Even when literal residence in the desert became impractical, the sayings of the Desert Fathers and Mothers, along with their community rules of poverty, chastity, obedience, fasting and prayer, became the basis for monastic life, which symbolically recreated the privations of the desert. The cultivation of simplicity by the Quakers and the Amish and of inner examination by Protestant pietists were similar attempts to forsake the distractions and temptations of materialism. The thirteenth-century German mystic Meister Eckhart taught that one should 'Be like a desert as far as the self and the things of this world are concerned' in order to discover the 'desert of the Godhead'.[15]

Giovanni Bellini,
St Jerome in the Desert,
c. 1480, oil on canvas.

Statue of Charles de
Foucauld in front of the
church of Saint-Pierre-
le-Jeune, Strasbourg.

Religious revivals in nineteenth-century Europe, fortuitously coinciding with the rise of escorted tourism (Thomas Cook undertook the first commercial tourist enterprise in 1841), led to a fascination with the deserts of the Holy Land, both as a living museum to illustrate the Bible and as a physical destination where, it was hoped, contact with the actual places where Jesus and his disciples had walked would revive and strengthen a simple faith, untroubled by the subversive arguments of contemporary science and history.[16] By the 1870s highly organized tours to Palestine were being conducted;[17] typically more than 1,000 Europeans were camped there at any one time, imbibing the religious 'atmosphere' of the desert.

Fascination with the promise of mystical experiences in the desert has persisted into modern times. At the beginning of the twentieth century Charles de Foucauld, a French cavalry officer, converted to the Catholic faith. Becoming first a Trappist monk and later a priest, he undertook a mission to live in the Sahara among the Tuareg in southern Algeria and write a dictionary of their language. He was shot dead in 1916 by Bedouin extremists resentful of the French presence in the Sahara, but his aim of initiating a religious institute was realized in 1933 with the founding of the Little Brothers of Jesus in French Algeria. A group of young French priests built a monastery in the oasis of El Abiodh, close to a Muslim pilgrimage centre.

Prior to the rise of Islam in the early seventh century, Arabian desert tribes followed a mixture of polytheistic practices and worship of astral deities, mingled with influences from Judaism and Christianity.[18] They maintained the value system that evolved from their nomadic existence, prizing honour, loyalty to the tribal leader, courage, hospitality and generosity. The person who changed this and substituted a rigid ideology was Muhammad, a poor man working in the caravan trade, who married Khadija, a rich widow and his former employer. Muhammad was a contemplative person given to solitary meditation on a hill near Mecca. On one occasion he believed he had been proclaimed the Messenger of God by the Archangel Gabriel. The Prophet, as he became known, received periodic revelations, which he later dictated from memory. These were finally collected as the Qur'an, which is believed by Muslims to complete earlier Jewish and Christian revelations and to be the direct and final word of God. The first principles of Islam are belief in a monotheistic God and submission to the will of Allah.[19]

Despite initial opposition to his ideas, Muhammad eventually became the most powerful military and religious figure of the area. Through his twelve subsequent marriages into various neighbouring desert tribes, by the time of his death in 630 CE he had united almost all of Arabia under Islam.

The intimate connections between Islam and its desert origins are recalled during the hajj, the pilgrimage to Mecca that all Muslims are expected to undertake at least once in their lifetime if they are physically and financially able to do so. Pilgrims walk seven times around the Kaaba in the courtyard of the Al-Haram Mosque. A central part of the hajj, the fifth pillar of Islam, commemorates the desperate search for water by Hagar. Abraham, at the demand of his first wife Sarah, had abandoned his second wife Hagar and her child Ishmael in the desert with only a small amount of food and water. When this ran out, Hagar laid the boy on the ground and, according to Islamic tradition, ran frantically between the hills of Safa and Marwah seven times, searching for water. When she prayed for help, God caused a spring to appear and this water source, the Well of Zamzam, still flows. As part of the hajj, pilgrims run seven times between the two hills, then drink water drawn from the well, symbolizing both their desert origins and their dependence on God for survival.

Although Muslims now regard the pre-Islamic era as the 'Age of Ignorance', they continue to revere the nomadic, desert values of that time, overlaid with a missionary zeal to spread Islamic beliefs worldwide. Since the Islamic conquest began in the seventh century, virtually all the desert nomads of North Africa have officially been Muslim, though they retain residual elements of pre-Islamic, desert-derived superstitions. Spirits of the desert winds are called *kel esuf* and feared as malevolent demons, ready to invade the unwary sleeper.[20] Hence, as we have seen, Tuareg men still wear tightly bound face veils to keep out evil jinns as well as the driving sand.

Native American desert peoples are also monotheists, believing in one Spirit who created all life. Thus all living things and the land itself are related, as members of a family, and have spirits. For the Navajo, the Apache and the Mojave this belief engenders the obligation to live in harmony with nature. Religious rites are conducted by shamans, who are believed to be endowed with magical abilities conferred through visions and dreams, and to be able to cure people through medicinal plants and cleansing rituals. Indeed, Apache religion has been described as 'devotional shamanism'.[21] The peyote cult that began in Mexico and spread to the people of Chihuahua and then other Native American tribes, based on the psychoactive effects of the alkaloid-producing cactus plant peyote, has attracted some Westerners to mystical/magical ceremonies involving visionary experiences, feats of endurance, fire dances, smoking ceremonies and communal trances. For Native Americans, however, the strictly prescribed practices of personal spirituality and communal ritual are not optional but

من وكَذَابِرَعَنِ الجَمَالِ الشَمَرَ وَانشَد

مَاالحَج مِبَرَكَ مَالَ وَدُنبَا وَادلاجَا وَلاالغَيَالِ الجَمَالُ الجَا وَاحدَلاجَا

obligatory, deriving directly from the exigencies of surviving in a harsh desert environment.

The Aboriginal Dreaming (a translation of the Aranda word *ulchurringa*, derived from *altjerri* 'to dream'[22]) is the oldest known continuous sacred tradition. Central to the Dreaming is the intimate bond between Aboriginal people and 'country'. This belief exists throughout the continent but is most striking in desert areas, which, to non-indigenous observers, appear bereft of life. Fundamental to the Aboriginal ideology and belief system is the inseparable connection between three sets of entities: the Ancestors, spirit beings who created and continue to nurture the

Al-Wasiti, *Group of Pilgrims on a Hajj*, 13th-century book illustration produced in Baghdad.

land in which they dwell; all the biological species, including humans, that they created; and the living, sustaining land. In this triad the land provides the vital nexus between the physical and the spiritual, between temporal and eternal, since, as the dwelling place of both supernatural beings and living creatures, it connects with both realms.

Several unique beliefs flow from this ideology. First, Australian Aborigines have no stories of alienation from nature equivalent to the account of the Fall in Genesis but regard themselves as an inseparable part of nature. Second, unlike most religious myths of origin, their creation stories locate the creative power deep within the land itself, not remotely in the heavens. During the Dreaming, a concept that expresses both a remote, past time and an eternally present time, mythical creative spirits emerged from the earth at locations that became the first sacred sites, endowed with the life and power of the supernatural entities.[23] In their epic journeys across the land these Ancestral Beings created the land-forms that remain permeated by their presence. Thus two ancestral sisters, crawling across the land, are believed to have imprinted a winding creek bed.[24]

After completing their creative acts, the Ancestral Beings sank back into the earth or transformed themselves into topographical features – rocks, trees, waterholes, clay pans, declivities – that,

The Kaaba at Masjid Al-Haram, the Grand Mosque at Mecca, during the start of hajj, 2008.

along with the sites of their particular exploits, are revered as continuing loci of supernatural power. Drawing on his lifelong experience with the Aranda peoples of central Australia, the anthropologist T.G.H. Strehlow wrote:

> In the scores of thousands of square miles that constitute the Aranda-speaking area there was not a single striking feature, which was not associated with an episode in one of the many sacred myths, or with a verse in one of the many sacred songs, in which aboriginal religious beliefs found their expression.[25]

These sites are surrounded by a circle of spiritual influence, the boundaries of which are known precisely to people of the area,[26] whose relationship with the spirit of the land is expressed in behavioural codes associated with the creation stories.

These landmarks are also visible reminders of the 'Law' laid down by the Ancestors and passed down through traditional observance. Like Judaic law, Aboriginal 'Law' or *tjukurpa* is a contract involving obligations to perform religious ceremonies, obey rules of behaviour and observe zones of avoidance associated with places or sights forbidden to particular age or gender groups.[27] In particular it involves responsibility to care for the land both physically (by keeping water holes and 'soaks' clear and regularly firing patches of bush) and spiritually (by performing the appropriate ceremonies to restore its fertility and honour the Ancestral Beings within it). In return the land nurtures them not only physically but spiritually, through the dance and song narratives of their tribal history, which recall and reenact their spiritual identity in connection to the earth.

For Aboriginal people the spirit world and the physical world coexist in continuous communication.[28] The physical world is not merely temporal and contingent; it has an eternal dimension demanding a personal I–thou relationship, rather than the I–it relationship accorded to inanimate objects. The latter attitude, in which response to the physical world involves only observation, measurement and exploitation, has characterized Western thinking since the Enlightenment. Thus for Aboriginal people the desert is not a wilderness but a place imprinted with spiritual meaning and riches invisible to the pragmatic and exploitative gaze of the colonists. As the Aboriginal poet Jack Davis wrote,

> Some call it desert
> But it is full of life
> Pulsating life
> If one knows where to find it
> In the land I love.[29]

In Australia during the twentieth century there arose a new interest and respect for Aboriginal spirituality. Associated pre-eminently with the central deserts, it provided a visionary alternative to both Western materialism and Christian orthodoxy, inspiring a range of diverse novels and poems that examine the desert as a site of spiritual presence. In 'Uluru, An Apostrophe to Ayers Rock', the poet Rex Ingamells, one of the first white Australians to use the Aboriginal place name, celebrated his empowerment at 'Uluru of the eagles' in the iconic centre of the desert:

> As I stepped out from one of your Caves of Paintings,
> I knew myself forever part of you,
> inspirited through ochre, charcoal and pipeclay,
> through aeons of ochre, charcoal and pipeclay,
> into your colourful darkness of timeless Being –
> yesterday, today and ever after
> eternal Dreaming in your heart, Uluru.[30]

The Aboriginal peoples who, until the 1980s, had been regarded by most white Australians as too primitive to embrace anything more than a misguided animism, have now been idealized as the guardians of eternal spiritual values that Western culture has allegedly lost in its pursuit of materialism. This belief permeated popular culture through films such as *Walkabout* (1971), in music and literature, and by the 1980s Australians began to realize that they could claim a vicarious source of ancient and transcendental desert experiences at the very heart of their continent.

This elevation of Aboriginal culture has been criticized as being merely appropriation by white Australians of desirable commodities – namely ancientness and environmentalism – that were lacking in their own relatively recent settler history. In *Edge of the Sacred* (1995) David Tacey points out that ascribing responsibility for the sacred to Aboriginal peoples may seem to be a mark of honour, but that in practice it perpetuates the existing racist hegemony. It disempowers white Australians spiritually but conveniently absolves them from responsibilities, and simultaneously precludes Aboriginal peoples from secular status and material wealth, thereby keeping them in a position of socio-economic subjection. 'The split is convenient but it is also fatal.'[31]

6 Travellers and Explorers

> No man can live this life [of a nomad] and emerge unchanged ...
> he will have within him the yearning to return ... For this cruel
> land can cast a spell which no temperate climate can match.
> Wilfred Thesiger, *Arabian Sands* (1959)

Deserts represent one of the few remaining frontier adventures.
Even though they have been traversed for centuries by indigenous, nomadic peoples, they still present the urban traveller with
physically demanding hardships, and perhaps a life-changing
experience. The immediate motivation of desert travellers may
be adventure, curiosity, scientific discovery, missionary zeal or the
desire to achieve some personal goal; but whatever the external
objectives, those who confront the challenge of solitude also
embark on an inner journey of self-discovery. No longer in control of their environment, they may undergo profound changes
in perception and self-awareness, achieving a liberation of spirit
and knowledge of their strengths and weaknesses. Such travellers
intrigue us by their tales of exotic regions, spiced with danger,
the accounts of their response to place and of the motivation that
drives them to risk their lives on long and difficult journeys.

Travellers are beholden to no one, but explorers carry with
them the hopes of others, often powerful others. Nevertheless,
beneath their overt goals of increasing national prestige, annex-
ing economic resources or expanding scientific knowledge,
explorers almost invariably have a personal agenda: a need for
increased self-esteem, heroism or fame, or the desire to be the first
to reach some geographic marker. For these reasons, explorers'
accounts retain our interest long after their discoveries have
been superseded by more advanced technology.

For the most part, desert explorers represent heroic failure:
they rarely reach their destinations, and, if they do, it may be in

circumstances that rob them of their triumph – Robert Falcon Scott's attempt to be the first to reach the South Pole was famously pre-empted by Roald Amundsen's arrival a mere 33 days before. Explorers who failed to achieve their goal, especially if they died in the attempt, are often honoured more highly in popular culture than those who succeeded in their aim. Readers may identify with their struggles against apparently insuperable odds and find them more heroic for their tragic failure.

This chapter focusses on a number of travellers and explorers in four desert regions: the Middle East, Central Asia, Australia and Antarctica. Though these areas are very diverse, the motivations and psychological responses of these visitors to the deserts they traversed were remarkably similar.

The Middle East

For centuries the lands lying between Eastern and Western civilizations have attracted articulate travellers, drawn there by religious pilgrimage, curiosity, military intrigues, personal challenge or the desire for solitude. All have contributed to the popular imagining of the desert.

Among the first written accounts is that of the Moroccan explorer Ibn Battuta (1304–c. 1368), who set out as a young man on his travels to Mecca and beyond, travels that were to last for 30 years. Journeying mainly with pilgrimage caravans comprising as many as 20,000 travellers, 'so many that the earth surged with them as the sea surges with dashing waves',[1] he always remained within the familiar cultural cocoon of Islam and the Arabic language and customs. On returning home to Morocco, Ibn Battuta then travelled south to Sijilmasa, a Berber trading post on the northern edge of the Sahara. From there he journeyed by camel caravan to Taghaza, a dry lakebed in present-day Mali where blocks of salt were dug and transported to the wealthy Malian capital. He was amazed to find that salt was sold for its weight in gold, or even multiples of that, depending on the market.[2] His recollections were recorded in the *Rihla* or 'Book of Travels', which remained unknown outside the Islamic world until translated by French scholars in the nineteenth century.

In modern times the first Westerner to explore the Middle East was the Swiss traveller and Orientalist Johann Ludwig Burckhardt. After studying Arabic and the Qur'an, he took up residence in Syria, disguised as a Muslim, and made expeditions into present-day Jordan. In 1812 he came upon the ancient city of Petra, capital of the Nabataeans, which had remained 'undiscovered' for a millennium. The buildings of this 2,000-year-old 'rose-red city half as old as time', as it was described in John William Burgon's poem 'Petra' (1845), are carved out of the sandstone of a towering rockface that can only be approached through a narrow canyon, the Siq. The most significant buildings in the city to have withstood the earthquake of 363 CE and the subsequent looting are Al Khazneh (the treasury) and Ad Deir (the monastery), but there are also royal tombs and an amphitheatre remaining from this wealthy centre of the spice trade in the first centuries BCE.[3] Burckhardt's descriptions, relayed to Britain, attracted artists, archaeologists and, more recently, film-makers. Later, disguised as a poor Syrian trader, Burckhardt made a dangerous pilgrimage to Mecca and then visited Medina. His daring feat was emulated by later British travellers in disguise, notably Sir Richard Burton in 1853 and Charles Doughty in 1876.[4] Doughty's monolithic *Travels in Arabia Deserta* (1888), a 1,200-page account of a two-year journey in present-day Saudi Arabia, was written in a unique convoluted style incorporating stylistic echoes of the King James Bible and the inflections and rhythms of Arabic overlaid on Latin constructions. His account of his journey begins:

> The new dawn appearing we removed not yet. The day risen the tents were dismantled, the camels led in ready to their companies, and halted beside their loads. We waited to hear the cannon shot which should open that year's pilgrimage.[5]

Doughty's narrative failed to excite his contemporaries but achieved brief popularity when T. E. Lawrence wrote a preface for the 1921 edition.

In the early twentieth century a new generation of travellers initiated a re-visioning of the Middle East not as a relic of antiquity but as a contemporary culture of strategic military importance. Prominent in this process were two English women from wealthy families, Gertrude Bell and Freya Stark, each of whom travelled alone, except for Arab servants. Their acquired knowledge and contacts with Arab sheiks became important in the development of British foreign policy, and during the First World War both were employed by the British Ministry of Information. Both were highly respected by the Royal Geographic Society (Bell was awarded its Gold Medal) and both were prolific and eloquent writers. Their travel books included accounts of the history and politics of the region as well as vivid descriptions of desert landscapes and Bedouin culture.

Gertrude Margaret Lowthian Bell CBE (1896–1926), writer, historian, political adviser, linguist (she was fluent in Arabic, Persian and Turkish as well as French, German and Italian), administrator and archaeologist, drew on her remarkable intellect, energy and determination to indulge her passion for adventure in the unmapped desert areas of Palestine, Syria and Arabia. Very few Westerners had penetrated to these remote places and most had never been visited by a European woman.[6] 'Looking like a Bedouin on her masculine saddle, dressed in her kafeeyah, coat and skirt . . . she rode off across the bare volcanic rocks of the Hauran plain, towards the territory of the Druze', isolated, warlike tribes living in the mountainous area of Jebel al-Druze.[7]

Beset with the double dangers of extreme desert conditions and warring tribal confederations, between whom it was necessary to negotiate safe passage, Bell believed that, 'since a woman can never disguise herself effectually . . . [her best defence was being] known to come of great and honoured stock, whose customs are inviolable'.[8] She therefore presented herself as a great lady, daughter of the 'paramount sheikh of Northern England'.[9] Included in her luggage were fine china tea services, crystal and silver, evening gowns and silks and lace for dining with sheiks, as well as cameras and guns, with the bullets hidden in her shoes.[10] Despite her unmistakable femininity, Bell was

Facade of Al Khazneh temple, Petra, Jordan.

treated by Bedouin sheikhs as an equal in discussing politics and world affairs.[11]

Non-judgemental about the tribal hierarchies and the perpetual raiding and counter-raiding of the Bedouin, she was fascinated by the empty spaces of the Arabian Desert. She sniffs the desert like a prisoner sensing release.

> The gates of the enclosed garden are thrown open, the chain at the entrance of the sanctuary is lowered, with a wary glance to right and left you step forth, and, behold! The immeasurable world. The world of adventure and of enterprise . . . an unanswered question and an unanswerable doubt hidden in the fold of every hill.[12]

In a diary entry that resonates with many desert travellers, she wrote:

> I think no one can travel here and come back the same. It sets its seal upon you, for good or ill . . . In spite of the desolation, and the emptiness, it is beautiful – or is it beautiful partly because of the emptiness?[13]

Through her knowledge of the area and the relations she forged with tribal leaders Bell played a pivotal role in events leading to the establishment of the modern state of Iraq.

Bell's contemporary Freya Stark (1893–1993) recorded that her fascination with the Middle East began on her ninth birthday, when she received a copy of *One Thousand and One Nights*, but she was 30 before she learned Arabic and travelled into the wilderness of western Iran, including areas where no Westerners had penetrated. A skilled cartographer, she mapped some of the most remote regions of Iran: the Elburz and Zagros Mountains and the Valleys of the Assassins. Stark was one of the first Western women to travel through the mountainous and dangerous Hadhramaut desert (now part of Yemen), as described in *The Southern Gates of Arabia* (1936).

Confident of her abilities, Stark created for herself a multifaceted reputation as nomadic traveller, social lioness, public

A view of Jebel Tuwaiq escarpment from the west; Riyadh lies just beyond the horizon. This was the area, in central Arabia to the north of the Rub' al Khali (Empty Quarter), where Gertrude Bell travelled to meet with the Druze.

servant, writer, cartographer and mythmaker. Unlike Bell, she gave considerable space in her writings to women, insisting on the power of the harem in a sheikh's policy-making. Although she writes mostly about people, her work includes memorable portrayals of landscape, like this description of the Hadhramaut plateau:

> The waters and the wind have worked, and the flat surface is eaten into and threatened on every side. The great ravines roll themselves down to Hajr, over an immense fan of eroded tortured lands. Here there is no water except what lies in pools of limestone below in shady places . . . To right and left . . . the uninhabited valleys fell away.[14]

Bell and Stark were contemporaries of the now more famous figure Thomas Edward Lawrence (1888–1935), a British army officer who liaised with the leaders of the Arab Revolt against Turkish rule. Lawrence, who had formerly been an archaeologist in northern Syria, was co-opted by the British Government in 1914 to make a military survey of the Negev Desert under cover of his archaeological work, since the Ottoman army would have to cross this area to attack Egypt. The British Foreign Office planned to divide the resources of the Ottoman Empire, an ally of Germany, by promoting and financing an Arab revolt against the Turks. Lawrence's knowledge of the desert and his fluency in Arabic were considered crucial to this plan, and in liaison with Emir Faisal, he organized strategic guerrilla attacks, including repeated bombing of the Hejaz Railway, a major supply line for Ottoman troops. His best-known achievements were a surprise overland attack on the strategic Turkish-held coastal town of Aqaba, previously considered impossible because of the desert crossing involved, and his part in the Allied capture of Damascus.

Recent revisionist assessments of Bell, Stark and Lawrence have criticized them as voyeuristic travellers who observed and then departed at will. Having constructed their version of the Orient, they felt they 'owned' it and that it should not change. The cultural studies critic Edward Said has asserted that these three shared 'great individuality, sympathy and intuitive identification with the Orient, a jealously preserved sense of personal mission in the Orient, cultivated eccentricity and final disapproval of the Orient. For them all, the Orient was their direct, personal experience of it.'[15]

Said would doubtless have included in this condemnation Wilfred Thesiger (1910–2003), who, after a distinguished career

Hadhramaut Valley, Yemen, where Freya Stark travelled.

as an explorer in Ethiopia and as a member of the Sudan Defence Force during the First World War, twice crossed the notorious Empty Quarter of the Arabian peninsula. In his book *Arabian Sands* (1959) he describes being struck by 'the patina of human history [that] was thick along the edges of the desert', where tribes 'claimed descent from Ishmael and listened to old men who spoke of events which had occurred a thousand years ago as if they had happened in their own youth'.[16] Thesiger's acknowledged motivation was threefold: to be first, to be famous, to be alone.

> The Empty Quarter . . . was one of the very few places left where I could satisfy an urge to go where others had not been . . . [It] offered me the chance to win distinction as a traveller; but I believed that it could give me more than this, that in those empty wastes I could find the peace that comes with solitude and, among the Bedu, comradeship in a hostile world.[17]

The Central Asian Deserts

Tashkent, Samarkand, Bukhara, Srinagar, Kandahar, Isfahan, Persepolis: for Europeans at the beginning of the twentieth century, these names of cities along the Silk Road resonated with romantic and literary associations from the past. But the rediscovery of the so-called Silk Road itself and the rich diversity of its cultural and linguistic history and archaeology were facilitated preeminently by Marc Aurel Stein, who made four major expeditions to Central Asia between 1900 and 1930. During his travels in Chinese Turkestan he covered some 40,000 km by pony or on foot, unearthing previously lost cities and forgotten languages as he retraced the Silk Road across the Lop Nur salt beds, 190 km of totally barren country without water, fuel or grazing for animals. Stein rediscovered the Jade Gate, marking the western extent of China, and recovered manuscripts in previously lost Tocharian languages of the Tarim Basin.

The Royal Geographical Society awarded Stein its Founder's Gold Medal for his expeditions into the Central Asian deserts

and he was knighted by the British government for his gift to the British Museum of many of the treasures he had removed from the Caves of the Thousand Buddhas, as described in chapter Four. By present-day standards Stein was an archaeological pirate, removing paintings, frescoes, statues and manuscripts, including the memoirs of Marco Polo and the T'ang monk Xuanzang. In mitigation it should be noted that the treasures he removed are now available to the world's scholars while many of those he left behind have since been lost or destroyed.[18]

Aurel Stein, 'My Companions and Myself at Ulugh-Mazar, in the Desert North of Chira'; Stein is centre front with his dog Dash, c. 1910.

Stein's Swedish contemporary, the geographer, explorer, cartographer, archaeologist and travel writer Sven Hedin (1865–1952), also made four expeditions into Central Asia, including the Tarim Basin and the Taklamakan Desert. His scientific expedition to Mongolia and Chinese Turkestan between 1927 and 1935 was like an invading army, involving 37 scientists, arms and 300 camels. In the Lop Nur desert Hedin discovered ruins indicating that the Great Wall of China had once extended to Xinjiang and on his recommendation the Chinese government constructed streets, irrigation systems and mines for coal, gold, iron and manganese, irrevocably changing the landscape of these once-remote areas.

In contrast to these two men, intent on scientific discoveries and archaeological spoils, some intrepid women travellers were drawn to these inhospitable deserts with very different motivations. Ella Maillart (1903–1997), Swiss skier, mountaineer, sailor and film-maker, yearned for adventure. Dismayed by the complexities and 'mad materialism' of interwar Europe, Maillart cherished a romantic desire to live with 'primitive, simple people' and rediscover 'elemental laws'. She was particularly attracted by the notion of 'solitude as old as the hills'.[19] While travelling to Samarkand, 'the fabled ruins of Tamerlane', she recited to herself lines from James Elroy Flecker's poem *Hassan*: 'For lust of knowing what should not be known / We take the Golden Road to Samarkand'. From there she trekked to Bukhara across the snow-covered Kyzyl Kum desert with 'nothing but grey sky and grey ice … grandiose in its desolation',[20] where her party had to cut and melt blocks of ice for water. Three years later she teamed up with Peter Fleming, correspondent for the London *Times*, for a seven-month journey of 5,600 km by train, lorry, foot, horse and camel from Peking to Srinagar in Kashmir to discover what was happening in the civil war in Chinese Turkestan. They had first to pass though the desolate Quaidam Basin, then cross the Taklamakan Desert via the old Silk Road.

For Maillart these journeys were at least partly to prove her physical and mental endurance and her ingenuity. She quoted Blaise Cendrars:

> Adventure is not … a romance … Adventure is always something lived through, and to make it part of oneself, the most important thing is to have proved worthy to live it, to live it without fear.[21]

Seemingly very different from all these travellers were three remarkable English women missionaries committed to bringing the Bible to western China. Yet the book of their experiences,

The Gobi Desert (1950) also shows their delight in this often dangerous adventure and in the developing trust and friendship of the local people. Educated in Geneva, Evangeline French (1869–1960) had been a young political radical before applying to join the China Inland Mission. Initially the missionary society found her too unconventional in her thinking and 'too fashionable' in her dress, but it finally assigned her to the Shanxi mission, where she was joined by Mildred Cable (1878–1952), who had studied pharmacy and human sciences at London University, and later by her sister Francesca French (1871–1960). In 1923 the three women applied to work in western China, then largely Muslim and relatively unknown in the West. Following the Hexi Corridor, they established a base in Jiuquan. From here they travelled some 2,400 km in thirteen years, evangelizing in Tibetan villages, Mongol encampments and Muslim towns throughout Xinjiang Province, distributing Bibles and Christian literature. They studied Uyghur in order to communicate with Muslim women and learned to be at home 'in a crowded *serai*, a Mongol *yurt*, a Siberian *isba*, a Chinese courtyard, a mud shack, a camel-driver's tent, or the palace of a Khan'.[22]

Evangeline and Francesca French and Mildred Cable, 1930s.

Unlike Stein and Hedin, who travelled in large caravans with armed guards, these indomitable women loaded their literature on to an unsprung donkey cart to journey along the Silk Road alone or with a carter, sometimes riding a donkey, sometimes on foot, following old trade routes. 'Five times we traversed the whole length of the desert, and in the process we had become part of its life' – and part of its silence.[23]

> The only sound was the steady quiet tramp of the animals' feet and the soft tread of the carter's cloth shoes . . . I had previously known great silences, but in comparison with this it seemed that they were noisy. There was not even a blade of grass to rustle, a leaf to move, a bird to stir in its nest . . . no one spoke, we only listened intently.[24]

The women were taken to shrines and temples normally hidden from foreigners. At the temple grottoes of Mati Si they saw shrines hollowed within a sandstone cliff with interconnecting rock stairways. Each cell, lit by small window, contained Indian-style figures wearing draperies and anklets never seen in a Chinese temple, and wooden statues of the Buddha flanked by elephants with trunks lifted in homage.

Alone in this immense desert, they learned the absolute necessity of keeping strictly to the faintly traced path made by previous travellers, and the danger of mirages in the form of 'glitter sand' or 'dust-demons' that seemed, from a distance, to walk slowly across the plain. Close up, these were cyclonic whirlwinds, lifting sand and rocks from the ground. They also learned to ignore the strange illusory sounds, like voices calling or camel bells, which lure the unwary traveller from the path.[25] Hearing of the enchanting beauty of the Lake of the Crescent Moon, they climbed the tiers of the Mingsha 'singing sands' that buried their feet to the ankle at every step to gaze down upon it.

> Small, crescent-shaped and sapphire blue, it lay . . . like a jewel in the folds of warm-tinted sand. On its farther shore stood a small temple surrounded with silvery trees,

and on the surface of the lake a flotilla of little black divers were swimming.[26]

At the end of her journeying in the Gobi, Cable wrote: 'The old desert fathers held that solitude is a thing to be earned, and on our long, slow journeys we knew that we were earning it.'[27] She also noted a feature of deserts that was to impress artists of the Australian deserts:

> The air is so clear that there is no perspective . . . every object stands out stereoscopically and with amazing clearness . . . [just as] the detachment of life from all normal intercourse imparts a sense of gravity to every rencontre . . . On a desert track there is no such thing as a casual meeting.[28]

The Taklamakan retains its allure. Charles Blackmore, a British army officer who had retraced over 1,000 km of

Crescent Lake, Dunhuang, in the Gobi Desert.

Lawrence's journeys in Arabia, still longed to revisit open desert spaces 'which offered a challenge: somewhere unknown, different, possibly uncharted and sufficiently remote to be hailed as breaking the last frontiers of exploration'.[29] In 1993, after difficult political negotiations with the Chinese, he assembled a party of British, Chinese and Uyghurs, equipped with 30 camels, to cross the Taklamakan from west to east. The distance of 1,250 km on the map was enormously extended by the need to traverse lines of north–south dunes, many of which towered over 300 m. Determined to achieve a 'first', Blackmore insisted on crossing the desert straight across the middle, rather than following the old trade routes along its northern and southern borders. As a result, the expedition incurred immense difficulties as exhausted men and beasts toiled up the steep dunes and heavily laden camels stumbled off ridges, dragging others down with them. Their survival depended on meeting supply teams that came in at several points along the route with water and food and provided new camels halfway across. Colonial-like,

Mingsha Singing Sands.

Blackmore recorded his intense delight at being the first to step here: 'No one had seen it before: it was mine. I was its conqueror and my footsteps would strip the virginity from the ruffled layers of sand that stretched unbroken and pure in front of me.'[30]

Though frequently split by personal and intercultural tensions, the expedition finally reached the eastern end of the desert after 60 days. They had discovered the ruins of a long-forgotten town, an ancient forest and shaped flints some 10,000 years old, suggesting that in prehistoric times the now arid Tarim Basin was a fertile valley occupied by hunter-gatherers. Sadly, the explorers' assiduous daily collection of sand samples for researchers at Oxford University proved futile, since the Chinese confiscated them in order to destroy any evidence of fallout from a nuclear device detonated in the Lop Nur Desert.

Australia

The travellers encountered thus far were not explorers in the strict sense. The areas they traversed had been familiar to local inhabitants for centuries and in most cases the travellers had indigenous people as guides. But Australia, like Antarctica, was 'new' in a different way. Although Australian Aborigines knew their country in minute detail, they were rarely consulted by British settlers, who had no concept of what lay beyond the coastal fringe. Inland exploration was driven by the need for agricultural and grazing land, but it was also a bid to compete with the British exploration of Africa. Ernest Giles was acutely aware of the comparison with his more famous counterparts, Burton, Speke and Livingstone. He emphasized the difficulty of his modest discoveries and hence, implicitly, the honour due to them:

> I have no Victoria or Albert Nyanzas, no Tanganyikas, Lualabas, or Zambezes, like the great African travellers to honour with Her Majesty's name, but the humble offering of a little spring in a hideous desert, which, had it surrounded the great geographical features I have enumerated, might

well have kept them concealed for ever, will not, I trust, be deemed unacceptable in Her Majesty's eyes.[31]

The European exploration of inland Australia, carried out over half a century through publicly funded expeditions, resulted largely in disappointment and significant loss of life. Yet although the colonists' hopes for well-watered grazing land were frustrated, the explorers created their own narratives, rewriting their journeys as feats of legendary courage by individuals pitted against a malevolent and treacherous country characterized by deceptive mirages and 'rivers' that rarely flowed. Reinventing themselves as heroic individuals, figures that a new nation was eager to acquire, they subtly changed the original goals of their expeditions, substituting endurance for economic benefit, exploit for exploration. Abortive forays and errors of judgement were edited out, leaving admiring readers with classic texts of heroic exploration that were to determine the nation's attitude to the central deserts for nearly a century.

The mythology of glorious failure began with Edward John Eyre's account of his epic journey across the southern coastal deserts in 1841, minimizing the fact that he survived by dint of some days' respite aboard a French ship that fortuitously lay at anchor off the coast. Four years later, Charles Sturt determined to be the first to unfurl the British flag at the centre of the continent. Believing himself preordained to discover the 'sacred mystery' of the interior, he set out from Adelaide in 1844, farewelled by optimistic colonists, to search for an inland sea with great rivers watering the interior. He did not reach the centre, and he was 120 million years too late for the vast Eromanga Sea that had occupied central Australia in the Cretaceous Era. Nevertheless, Sturt wrote himself into the explorers' hall of fame with a narrative that reads like the first Australian gothic novel. Blockaded by drought at Depot Glen, he internalized his physical detention as a psychological prison, describing his party as prisoners 'locked up in the desolate and heated region . . . as effectively as if we had wintered at the Pole'.[32] The 30-metre-high parallel sand dunes of the Simpson Desert 'rose up in

S. T. Gill, *Captain
Charles Sturt Leaving
Adelaide*, 1844, drawing.

terrible array against us . . . succeeding each other like waves of
a tempestuous sea'.[33]

Sturt's failure was followed by the complete disappearance of
Ludwig Leichhardt's second expedition somewhere in the centre
of Australia around 1848. The figure of 'lost Leichhardt', an
experienced German explorer and scientist, provided a rich source
of speculation and fictional reconstruction, setting the stage for
Australia's most theatrical and disastrous expedition, led by Robert
O'Hara Burke and William Wills. Departing from Melbourne in
1860, they attracted 15,000 spectators, who came to marvel at the
exotic camels, mountains of baggage (including a whale boat for
sailing on the assumed inland sea) and unprecedented length of
the cavalcade.[34] A year later, Burke, Wills and five other members
of the nineteen-man expedition were dead as a result of misdirec-
tion and poor judgement. Yet for decades Burke's reputation as
heroic leader remained unquestioned. These 'failed' explorers
provided the nation with a cathartic sense of greatness, of high
tragedy, with the desert as malicious antagonist. At their state
funeral, which was held on a scale rivalling that of royalty, the
40,000 attendees were not merely mourning Burke and Wills
but celebrating the nation's first martyrs.

So pervasive was the association between fame and death
that explorers who succeeded in their missions and returned

alive were relegated to secondary status. John McDouall Stuart, who did reach the centre of the continent and whose route became the path of the vital telegraphic link between north and south, Ernest Giles, arguably the greatest inland explorer in terms of distance covered and endurance, Augustus Gregory, Peter Warburton and John Forrest are far less well known and celebrated than their unsuccessful counterparts.

Because the desert experience was, for nearly a century after these expeditions, unavailable to others, the explorers' narratives provided fiction writers with the ready-made imagery of a nightmare landscape embodying the deepest fears of European colonists: drought, thirst, loneliness, alienation and death in a strange land. Their hatred of the desert was indelibly inscribed on the map: Mt Disappointment, Mt Despair, Mt Destruction, Mt Deception, Mt Desolation, Mt Misery, Mt Barren, even the Ophthalmia Range.

Despite twentieth-century modes of transport, the Australian desert continued to issue a challenge for individuals seeking one, such as Robyn Davidson. In 1977 Davidson travelled 2,700 km solo across the Western Desert from Alice Springs to the Indian Ocean with four camels, driven by an inner compulsion to prove herself. Her very successful account of her journey, *Tracks* (1980), was particularly popular with female readers, who respected Davidson's undertaking such a journey of her own volition and, for most of the time, alone. The book played a significant role in the emerging neo-Romantic cult of the desert as a space for enlightenment and self-discovery.

Antarctica

Because there were no indigenous peoples in Antarctica it was the only continent to be truly 'discovered' by Europeans. Although the Russian Captain Bellingshausen had sighted the Antarctic mainland in 1820 and twice circumnavigated it, Antarctica at the beginning of the twentieth century was still largely unknown. The last frontier, the ultimate desert in size, remoteness and extreme conditions, its exploration was the space race of the decade. A resolution of the Sixth International Geographical Congress in London in 1895 urged all scientific societies to press for exploration of the Antarctic regions,[35] effectively firing the starting pistol for the race to the geographical South Pole. Belgian, English, French, Scottish and Norwegian expeditions competed for the honours.

The contest ended when Roald Amundsen's Norwegian party reached the Pole in December 1911, followed just 33 days later by Robert Scott's British team, but this did not deter future explorers. The men involved in these exhausting expeditions of the 'heroic age' of Antarctic exploration became legendary figures, depicted as doggedly pursuing a manly, patriotic ideal or the noble cause of science even though at least some, like the Australian inland explorers of the previous century, were motivated by hopes of promotion or fame. Ernest Shackleton gave as his reasons love of adventure, scientific knowledge and fascination with the unknown, adding, '[T]he stark polar lands grip the hearts of men who have lived on them in a manner that can hardly be understood by the people who have never got outside the pale of civilization.'[36] Amundsen quoted his mentor, Fridtjof Nansen: 'A victory of human mind and human strength over the domination and powers of Nature.'[37] Acquiring scientific knowledge was the justification for the cost and danger involved as numerous parties set out to map the coastline and islands, monitor the (shifting) location of the South Magnetic Pole, explore the Polar Plateau and the Great Ice Barrier, cross the continent and collect data about climate, biology and geology.

These early expeditions were small and conducted on a shoestring budget, without the sophisticated accessories and back-up support that can now be instantaneously summoned by satellite video conferencing. Gear was heavy and clumsy, and transport depended on dogs or man-hauling of heavy sledges. Teams could carry only minimal supplies and their navigation instruments were adversely affected by proximity to the magnetic pole.

By objective criteria, Scott's two South Polar expeditions were a debacle. In the first he lost at least one man through negligence, and almost lost his ship *Discovery* in the ice. Yet when he and his men reached England in 1904 they were greeted as heroes by a nation that, in the face of self-doubts arising from Darwinism and exacerbated by defeats in the Boer and Crimean wars, needed to bolster belief in British racial superiority.[38] Scott's second expedition of 1911–12 was an even greater disaster. Having lost the race to the Pole, his entire polar party died on the return journey. Yet his diary depicted a team of heroic individuals confronting insuperable odds, self-sacrificing to the last. To Scott's contemporaries, brought up on adventure tales from the *Boy's Own Annual* and not yet made cynical by a world war, his narrative was a jewel in the crown of British imperialism. However, as in the case of the Australian explorers, a brutal revisioning process followed. In 1985 journalist Roland Huntford shocked the English-speaking public by suggesting that Scott had bullied his men and manipulated history. Scott's reputation was rapidly transferred from event to literary achievement. American novelist Ursula Le Guin remarked, 'Because he was an artist his testimony turns mere waste and misery into that useful thing, tragedy.'[39]

By contrast, the Australian geologist and explorer Douglas Mawson was not interested in the scramble to the Pole, but only in scientific research.[40] He successfully led the first Australasian Antarctic Expedition (1911–14), carrying out geological, biological and meteorological observations and mapping large areas of the coastline. Accompanied by the Swiss Xavier Mertz, a champion skier and mountaineer, and Lieutenant Belgrave Ninnis, Mawson led an expedition to explore the area east of Adélie Land. When Ninnis and one of the dog teams were lost down a crevasse with most of their supplies 500 km from their hut, Mawson and Mertz set off to walk back to the base, gradually eating the remaining sled dogs and, finally, hauling their own sled. Mertz died 160 km from the base, leaving Mawson, weak from lack of food, to struggle on alone. Delayed for a week by a raging blizzard, he finally reached the base camp only to see the expedition ship departing north for the winter. Sir Edmund Hillary later described this lone journey back to the base as 'probably the greatest story of lone survival in Polar exploration'.[41] Unfortunately his vivid account, *Home of the Blizzard* (1915), was submerged in the tide of mourning for Scott and the tragedy of the First World War.

The fourth 'heroic' leader, Ernest Shackleton, after two un-successful attempts on the Pole, turned his attention to another 'first': crossing Antarctica via the Pole. Despite meticulous prepar-ations he was defeated by the weather when his ship *Endurance* was frozen in the Weddell Sea. Shackleton masterminded a heroic rescue of all his men, sailing through mountainous seas in an open boat and crossing the mountain chain of South Georgia to reach the Norwegian whaling station at Grytviken for help.

Very different from this 'heroic age' of Antarctic discovery were the American expeditions of Richard E. Byrd. Using aeroplanes, aerial cameras, snowmobiles and elaborate com-munications devices,[42] his first expedition (1928–30) completed large-scale aerial mapping and survey work, meteorological observations and geological surveys. In his second expedition (1933–5) Byrd aimed to record continental, rather than coastal, weather. The weather station at Bolling Advance Base was built 180 km inland on the Ross Ice Shelf. Here, for four and a half months of an Antarctic winter, Byrd chose to remain alone in a hut measuring 3 m × 4.5 m, recording meteorological and aurora observations. Inspired by Thoreau's sojourn at Walden Pond, he intended 'to taste peace and quiet and solitude long enough to find out how good they really are',[43] and to catch up on books, music and philosophy. Byrd's observations have passed into statistics but the book he later wrote, *Alone* (1938), has become a classic of literature, both for its evocative descriptions of the brilliant spectacle of auroras and for the account of his interior journey during these months of darkness and solitude. Byrd experienced a deep sense of cosmic harmony, of an 'all-pervading intelligence', and a conviction that the human race is not an acci-dent but 'as much part of the universe as the trees, the mountains, the aurora, and the stars'.[44] This euphoria was cut short by carbon monoxide poisoning from the oil-burning stove. Byrd became weaker and sank into depression, then despair. Fearing for his safety, his support team sent out a rescue mission, but for years he could not admit to the rescue, which he saw as evidence of failure on his part.

The recorded responses of these explorers to Antarctica were remarkably similar. Beginning with a sense of exhilaration at their imagined freedom from the restrictions and conventions of society, and awed by the magnificence of the towering icebergs they encountered on their voyage south, they arrived full of eagerness to prove themselves against the elements. But the Romantic notion of living amid snow and ice, cut off from the rest of the world, proved in the event monotonous, and ultimately melancholic. Charles Laseron, a member of Mawson's expedition of 1911–14, wrote of the depression caused by visual immensity:

> I hate this icy plateau . . . it is tremendously oppressive. It's too big, never-ending, day after day the same white expanse of utter absolute desolation and death. Nothing alive except ourselves and even this it somehow seems to resent. It is a great relief to get inside the tent and get some finality of vision.[45]

The spectacular scenery of Antarctica, now familiar through colour photography, impressed for a time but even the dramatic

Rear-Admiral Richard Byrd revisits his old hut site of Little America II in 1947. He is smoking tobacco in a corncob pipe, both of which had been left at the camp in 1935. This photo was taken during the u.s. Navy's Operation Highjump expedition.

Slant sastrugi,
Antarctica.

coloured light show of the aurora australis and the infinite vari-
ations of sculptured ice became overshadowed by the struggle to
survive. Sastrugi – long wavelike ridges of snow formed by winds,
usually several metres high and parallel to the prevailing wind
direction – impeded their progress as the dunes of sand deserts had
hindered other explorers; blizzards, like sandstorms, made travel
impossible and left behind a changed landscape with no recognizable markers; ice blink, the intense white glow seen at the horizon
resulting from reflection of light off an ice field beyond,[46] was
as unsettling as mirages caused by shimmering heat; treacherous

crevasses hidden by snow or thin ice brought instant death without trace; sensory deprivation in a whited-out world and the almost total absence of other life forms for most of the year induced deep depression. Charles Harrisson, another member of Mawson's expedition, wrote, 'All this land is Death . . . it might have been the graveyard of centuries, it looked so old.'[47]

Nevertheless, the heroic age of Antarctic exploration still inspires emulation. In 2007 Tim Jarvis, Anglo-Australian adventurer and environmental scientist, re-enacted Mawson's 1912 expedition, hauling a sled 500 km with the same minimal rations that Mawson had, to decide if Mawson's story was physically possible. Accompanied by John Stoukalo, who represented Xavier Mertz, until the exact point where Mertz died, Jarvis had to battle negative thoughts and deep depression to continue through blizzards to the end of the journey.[48]

On 23 January 2013 Jarvis set out with five others in the *Alexandra Shackleton*, a replica of Shackleton's lifeboat the *James Caird*, to relive that explorer's open-boat journey of 1,300 km from Elephant Island across the Southern Ocean to South Georgia. He and a companion then made the three-day mountain trek across vast snowfields and the steep Crean Glacier, then down almost vertical scree gullies to the old whaling station at Stromness, arriving on 10 February.[49] In both expeditions, Jarvis used only the materials and equipment his predecessors had. When asked why he put himself in such danger, Jarvis replied, 'For the physical challenge, to find out more about myself and what these old explorers went through.'[50]

The motives given for engaging with deserts, whether hot, cold or frozen, have included scientific curiosity and self-testing, but another may be to experience the sense of being overwhelmed by the power and vastness of nature. It is the accounts of such intense experiences, whether Romantic ecstasy or Gothic dread, that generate the unique allure of travels in deserts and ice and inspire writers and film-makers to create the fictional deserts of our imagination.

Gustave Doré, 'The Ice was All Around', illustration for *The Rime of the Ancient Mariner*, 1876, wood engraving.

7 Deserts of the Imagination

... Death has no repose
Warmer and deeper than that Orient sand
Which hides the beauty and bright faith of those
Who made the Golden Journey to Samarkand.
James Elroy Flecker, 'The Golden Journey to Samarkand' (1913)

Fascinating as the narratives of explorers and travellers are, it is the deserts of the imagination that engage us most and remain in our memory. Percy Bysshe Shelley's 'Ozymandias' (1818) expresses through its depiction of the Sahara our deepest fears of extinction; Flecker's 'Golden Journey to Samarkand' (1913) conjures up the powerful appeal of the Arabian desert; and Samuel Coleridge, who had never crossed the Channel when he wrote 'The Rime of the Ancient Mariner' (1798), produced the most evocative lines in the language about the Antarctic. Shelley's poem was written in response to news of the discovery of a colossal statue of Rameses II, which he had not yet seen.[1]

I met a traveller from an antique land
Who said: 'Two vast and trunkless legs of stone
Stand in the desert. Near them on the sand,
Half sunk, a shattered visage lies ...
And on the pedestal these words appear:
"My name is Ozymandias, King of Kings:
Look on my works, ye mighty, and despair!"
Nothing beside remains. Round the decay
Of that colossal wreck, boundless and bare,
The lone and level sands stretch far away.'[2]

Coleridge was inspired by tales he had heard at school from his mathematics master William Wales, who had been the astronomer aboard Captain Cook's ship *Resolution* when it sailed to the highest southern latitude then reached by any ship.[3] Coleridge read many other explorers' accounts before writing 'The Rime of the Ancient Mariner' and included their impressions of their journeys, even their words and phrases,[4] but the Mariner's experience of the ice has a unique Gothic power that mesmerizes us as it did the Wedding Guest, suggesting the poet's direct contact with one who had been there. Apart from his arbitrary and shocking act of killing the albatross, the Mariner is passive in his own story: events happen to him; we might even say landscapes 'happen' to him. In the Antarctic section the ice is the actor: it moves, it gleams, it makes fearful sounds and it is all-encompassing.

> And ice, mast-high, came floating by,
> As green as emerald.

> And through the drifts the snowy clifts
> Did send a dismal sheen: . . .

> The ice was here, the ice was there,
> The ice was all around:
> It cracked and growled, and roared and howled,
> Like noises in a swound![5]

Deserts of all kinds have exerted a hold on the Western imagination, as expressed in fiction and film. In these media, the desert functions as code for extreme physical conditions, for isolation and introspection, or for the place where the expectations of civilized society no longer hold. Such estrangement from our surroundings terrifies us with foreboding, as expressed in Flecker's poem 'Song of the East Gate Warden', where the Desert Gate of Damascus is described as 'Postern of Fate, the Desert Gate, Disaster's Cavern, Fort of Fear'.[6] It may elicit heroism or, more rarely, invite a visionary experience. Writers seeking realistic settings relied at first on explorers' accounts of the terrain; hence, inevitably, the desert was depicted antagonistically, as the self-justifying narratives of explorers and travellers, edited for public scrutiny, became the facts of fiction. Even now the desert is rarely subject; it is the enemy, the 'Other' to both the individual and civilization. Four shaping concepts in the portrayal of deserts will be explored here: adventure and romance, nationalism, Gothic horror and spiritual epiphany.

Adventure and Romance

The desert epitomizes life at the edge, where death awaits the traveller: either instantaneous death, caused by wild animals or villainy, or more lingering death, caused by exposure to nature. The external dangers of heat, thirst or, in the case of Antarctica, intense cold, and the ever-present risk of being disoriented and lost in a sand storm or blizzard, provide limitless opportunities for action, but may also initiate internal adventures as privation, solitude or imminent death evoke terror, self-discovery or revelation.

The first English adventure novel involving the desert was H. Rider Haggard's *King Solomon's Mines* (1885), which laid down the basic parameters for the 'lost world' genre: a map, a desert crossing, perilous mountains, lost civilizations and attacks from treacherous villains. Haggard had been hard pressed to find settings 'unknown to the pestilential accuracy of the geographer',[7] where adventure tales involving fictitious races could be located. He settled on Africa but later writers were to embrace Central Australia and Antarctica for the same purpose.

Nevertheless, the Sahara has retained a special place in the imagination of Europeans, partly because, for so long, it was the only desert they knew, and partly because of its long cultural history. P. C. Wren's bestseller *Beau Geste* (1924), set largely in French North Africa, follows three aristocratic English brothers who have joined the Foreign Legion for motives of loyalty, honour and self-sacrifice. The adventure stems less from the desert than from human drama – mutiny, desertion and attacking Tuaregs who are held at bay by two surviving Europeans propping up corpses at the fort's embrasures and firing from behind them. The desert is not romanticized, but functions as a scene of desolation and hardship that elicits courage and endurance from the British heroes. To the jaundiced eye of the commanding officer,

> There was beauty neither in the landscape nor in the eye
> of the beholder. The landscape consisted of sand, stone,
> *kerengia* burr grass, *tafusa* underbrush, yellow, long-stalked
> with long thin bean-pods . . . And across all the *Harmattan*
> was blowing hard, that terrible wind that carries the Saharan
> dust a hundred miles to sea . . . filling the eyes, the lungs,
> the pores of the skin, the nose and throat . . . rendering life
> a burden and a curse.[8]

The continuing popularity of this romance is apparent from the succession of film and television versions of *Beau Geste*, which appeared in 1926, 1939, 1966 and 1982.

In the 1920s the Sahara also became a popular location for romances involving Arab rebels, who replaced European colonists as heroes. Romberg and Hammerstein's operetta *The Desert Song* (1926) drew on the uprising in 1925 of the Riffs, Moroccan freedom fighters who opposed French occupation. Like two silent films of the period, *The Sheik* (1921) and *Son of the Sheik* (1926), both of which starred the Hollywood idol Rudolph Valentino, it featured a stereotyped Orientalist desert, exotic costumes, Bedouin riders and suggestions of harems.

A darker side of the colonial impact on traditional desert people is presented in *Désert* (1980) by the Nobel Prize-winning novelist J.-M.G. Le Clézio. A band of dispossessed Tuareg struggles through the Sahara, endlessly 'following the almost invisible trail' but arriving nowhere.

> The sand swirled about them, between the legs of the camels,
> lashing the faces of the women, who pulled the blue veils
> down over their eyes . . . The camels growled and sneezed.
> No one knew where the caravan was going . . .
> There was nothing else on earth, nothing, no one. They
> were born of the desert, they could follow no other path . . .
> They had been as mute as the desert for so long, filled with

the light of the sun burning down ... and frozen with the
night and its still stars ...

The routes were circular, they always led back to the
point of departure, winding in smaller and smaller circles
... But it was a route that had no end, for it was longer
than human life.[9]

By contrast with these fictional accounts, Antoine de Saint-
Exupéry's *Wind, Sand and Stars* (1939) was based on the author's
real-life adventures. As an Aéropostale pilot, he and his navi-
gator had crash-landed in the Sahara between Benghazi and
Cairo and spent many days and nights searching for water until,
almost dead from thirst, they were rescued by Bedouin. Despite
its dangers and hardships, Saint-Exupéry experiences in the
desert a joy he has felt nowhere else, a vision of life integrally
related to nature.

I lay there pondering my situation, lost in the desert and in
danger, naked between sky and sand ... I was no more than
a mortal strayed between sand and stars, conscious of the
single blessing of breathing ...

... This sea of sand bowled me over. Unquestionably it
was filled with mystery and danger. The silence that reigned
over it was not the silence of emptiness but of plotting, of
imminent enterprise ... Something half revealed yet wholly
unknown had bewitched me.[10]

Adventure films set in the Egyptian Sahara often implement
the danger and action intrinsic to the desert by reviving ancient
superstitions. The Indiana Jones film *Raiders of the Lost Ark*
(1981) involves a race against Nazis to acquire the Ark of the
Covenant, which supposedly contains invincible powers that will
lead to their world domination. *The Mummy* (1999), a remake of
the 1932 Boris Karloff film of that name, exploits superstitions
associated with the Egyptian dead, including an ancient curse
that eventually falls upon the villains. Supplementary dangers are
provided by Bedouin attacks, flesh-eating scarabs and the revived

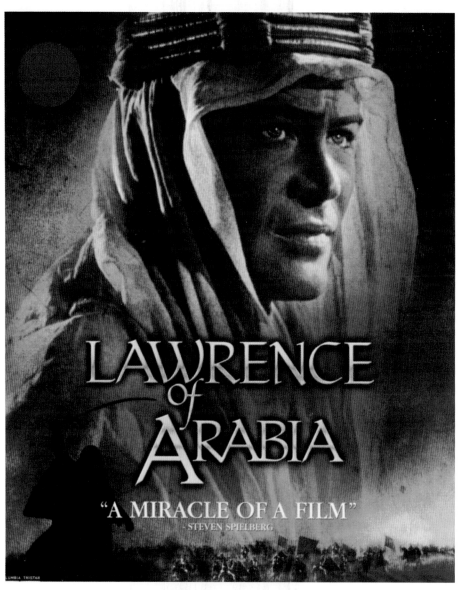

Poster for the film *Lawrence of Arabia* (dir. David Lean, 1962).

Poster for *The Mummy*
(dir. Stephen Sommers,
1999).

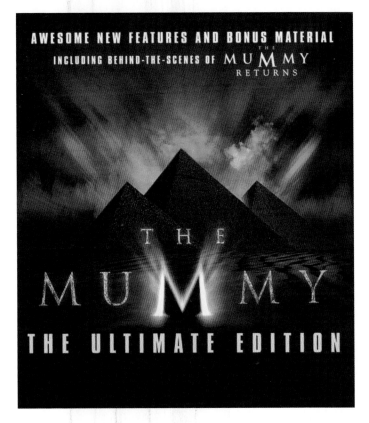

mummy Imhotep. Special effects turned the minimal plot into a blockbuster adventure movie that warranted four sequels involving the Scorpion King, an Egyptian cult, scorpion-filled pits and intervention from Anubis. In these films, as in *Sahara* (2005), the plot is tenuously linked to a distant past, importing superstition and magic, along with hostile Bedouin, to supplement the dangers and difficulties of nature.

Petra, the long-hidden city of the Nabataeans carved into the rock face of Wadi Araba, has also attracted film-makers. Its 'Treasury' features in the climactic scene of *Indiana Jones and the Last Crusade* (1989) as the entrance to the final depository of the Holy Grail, and the Monastery of Petra (Ad Deir) appears in *Transformers: Revenge of the Fallen* (2009) as the hidden tomb of the Primes. Like the pyramids or the Sphinx, Petra functions as a recognizable monument – as code for desert rather than as desert per se – facilitating the film-maker's need to indicate a desert place that is otherwise featureless and anonymous.

The desert also provides a place where more complex heroes emerge – and fall. The outstanding film example is David Lean's Academy Award-winning *Lawrence of Arabia* (1962), which purports to explore the psychology of a real-life adventurer courting death, the British agent who 'goes native'. In Lean's film the terrifying Nefud Desert, considered the 'worst desert in the world' even by Bedouin, is a character in its own right. In places it is red sand with black pyramidal rocks; at other times its straw-coloured sand, blown into knife-edged drifts, penetrates everything and Bedouin ride with their veils tightly wound around their faces, leaving only their eyes showing. But the desert is also pivotal in transforming the misfit Private Lawrence into Lawrence the hero. On receiving his commission to assess the prospects of Prince Feisal against the Turks, he exclaims, 'This is going to be fun.' The chief of the Arab Bureau replies tartly, 'Only two kinds of people get fun out of the desert – Bedouin and gods; and you, Lawrence, are neither.' But Lawrence believes he is both. The desert catapults him to semi-divine status as 'El Aurens' with his Bedouin admirers. In this role he parades majestically in white sharifi robes with gold dagger, alone against the background of the desert, acting the part of a tribal prince, or mounted on a camel, leading 'his' Arabs against the Turks. After crossing the Nefud by night to Aqaba, he finds that one of his companions has slipped off his camel. Defying all warnings, he risks his life to return for him by day, winning the devotion of the Bedouin. When an American reporter asks him what the attraction of the desert is, Lawrence replies, 'It's clean.' But Lawrence is also an anti-hero. Although the desert elicits from him superhuman feats of bravery, endurance and compassion, it is also his 'heart of darkness' where, removed from the restraints of 'civilization', he discovers a cathartic delight in acts of inhuman violence and brutality. Aroused by executing a man, he sets on a party of retreating Turks in an orgy of killing that appals even his Arab followers.

War and death in the desert feature again in *The English Patient* (1992), Michael Ondaatje's Booker Prize-winning novel (filmed in 1996). Although set largely in Italy, it includes crucial flashbacks to the Sahara at the onset of the Second World War. From these it becomes apparent that the unnamed 'Patient', burned beyond recognition, is not English but the Hungarian count László de Almásy, who led an archaeological survey and, like the real-life Almásy, discovered the ancient Cave of the Swimmers in Wadi Sura (discussed in chapter Four). In contrast to the idyllic painted scenes in the cave, the desert becomes the setting for violence. When Geoffrey Clifton, the husband of Almásy's lover, deliberately crashes his plane, killing himself and seriously injuring his wife Katharine, Almásy settles her in the cave and embarks on an exhausting trek across the desert for help. However, in British-controlled Cairo, a dehydrated and incoherent foreigner with a Hungarian name is immediately imprisoned. When Almásy eventually returns to the cave Katharine is dead from starvation and dehydration. These flashbacks offer memorable, visual insights into the beauty and terror of the desert, on to which are superimposed the tragedy of relationships and the brutality of war.

The road movie genre, derived from the picaresque novel – a series of encounters and adventures linked only by the presence of the travelling protagonist – has also frequently employed a desert location. This convention was prefigured some 1,500 years ago in the pre-Islamic odes or *Mu'allaqāt* of Arabia. These typically recount a brief stop by nomadic travellers at the site of some ruins where separate narratives of past events are recounted before the riders move on.[11] In the new, independent Arab cinema however, the Bedouin no longer live in the desert but travel through it on asphalt highways, the legacy of national, oil-derived wealth. Having traded their camels for cars, they drive aimlessly between towns as their ancestors once journeyed purposefully between oases for water and trade. Since the government-ordered settlement of Bedouin in towns, Arab movies are about leaving the desert, not living in it. The characters suffer endless delays, obstacles and wrong turns and rarely, if ever, arrive at their intended destination. They symbolize the waves of refugees washing around the world, especially in the war-torn Middle East. Typical of such frustrating journeys are the Lebanese road movie *Baalbeck* (2001) and the Iraqi film *Baghdad On/Off* (2002). A similar, arbitrary sequence of events characterizes *Wanderers of the Desert* (1986) by the Tunisian film-maker Nacer Khemir. It tells the story of a schoolteacher sent to a remote desert village where the people are obsessed with a story of buried treasure and children are believed to be under a curse to wander the desert. Strange mythical figures materialize, children are hurried through labyrinthine underground corridors, the teacher disappears, a ship is mysteriously washed up in the desert. All these non sequiturs become plausible against the mirage-like backdrop of the Tunisian desert, which, Khemir says, is a character in itself.

In Wim Wenders's classic desert road movie *Paris, Texas* (1984), Travis Henderson walks straight off the freeway into the vast South Texas desert, losing himself, his speech and his identity. Having driven his wife Jane away and abandoned his son, he seeks to erase his personality in the desert. However, his brother finds him and brings him to his home, where he is reunited with his son. The two set out again to find Jane. Henderson reconnects mother and son but drives off alone, the eternal wanderer, never divulging his destination. In all these films the desert plays a pivotal role in rendering credible otherwise arbitrary events with no apparent causal connection.

A very different desert encounter is presented in *The Adventures of Priscilla, Queen of the Desert* (1994). This colourful and atypically upbeat road movie follows three drag queens who set out from Sydney in a bus they name 'Priscilla, Queen of the Desert' to perform in Alice Springs, in the centre of the continent. After travelling through hostile, homophobic outback towns, through Aboriginal communities, who applaud their performance, and through the red sands of the Simpson Desert, they finally achieve the long-time ambition of one of the group: to stand on the cliffs of spectacular Kings Canyon in full transvestite rig. Against the immensity of the desert landscape, which both dwarfs and dignifies individuals, these indomitable travellers recover their selfhood.

Nationalism

Despite their initial refusal to believe that the centre of their continent was not fertile land but desert, both North American and Australian settlers eventually embraced their deserts as integral to their identity. In North America the colonists, battling for survival in the wilderness of the southwest, found nothing attractive in this harsh land. Only after mechanization and technology made it accessible, and an intriguing contrast to the densely populated cities, could an aesthetic appreciation of the American desert emerge. The first expression of this came from John Van Dyke, an asthmatic art historian and critic who was seeking dry air for his health. *The Desert* (1901), his account of the deserts of California and Arizona, was a turning point in appreciation of such landscapes. He writes of 'the majesty of it, the eternal strength of it, the poetry of its wide-spread chaos, the sublimity of its lonely desolation ... a landscape all color, a dream landscape.'[12]

Later nostalgia for the pioneering days found expression in westerns, which idealized courage, resourcefulness and individualism, qualities which became identified with the American character. Originally romantic tales of life in the Old West, they quickly became myths of nationalism, of America's 'manifest destiny', glorifying the bravery and freedom of the pioneers' pre-industrial lifestyle. The stock characters of westerns, itinerant cowboys or gunmen, are the counterparts of desert nomads, riding horses rather than camels between the oases of minimalist towns or cattle ranches and identified by a Stetson instead of a *keffiyeh*. In westerns the desert signifies danger, both from the desolate landscape and from outlaws, and the plot typically involves maintaining law and order against a range of forces that threaten stability – originally Native Americans, later bandits from south of the border.

The first (silent) epic western was *The Covered Wagon* (1923), which glorified the pioneers' wagon trains as they moved

westward, encountering such hazards as flooded river crossings, prairie fires, attacks by Indians and cattle stampedes. As well as action, westerns also present dramatic desert scenery. John Ford, one of the most famous directors of westerns, favoured the spectacular red mesas and buttes in the desert country of Monument Valley declaring, 'The real star of my westerns has always been the land.' Arguably, Monument Valley has defined what generations of moviegoers think of when they imagine the American West.

The central Australian deserts have also served to promote a national identity, even though the vast majority of the population, settled along the coastline, has never been there. In the 1880s and '90s the desert was almost an obligatory setting for adventure stories, 'ripping yarns' in which youthful protagonists, exemplifying the nation's manhood, conquered the land, discovering hidden gold mines, encountering cannibal tribes or stumbling upon the secret of vanished explorers modelled on Ludwig Leichhardt.[13] These successful fictional heroes both overwrote the failures of the nation's real explorers a generation earlier, and distinguished themselves from the timid, effete English characters in these novels, to create and celebrate a new colonial

View of Monument Valley between Arizona and Utah, symbol of the Wild West and setting for many John Ford westerns.

identity. Stumbling upon a gold reef or even a gold mountain was a popular theme, influenced partly by Rider Haggard's successful formula but also playing upon the immigrant's dream of immense and instant riches. These adventurers also encounter ancient civilizations and defeat hostile foreign tribes, Asian or African in origin, who represent the nation's suppressed nightmares of hybridization and degeneracy through infiltration of Asian races.[14] In these novels the desert provides not only testing conditions and a licence for fantastic scenarios but, through its location at the centre of the continent, the symbol of the nation's innermost self and pervasive fears of invasion.[15]

With independence from Britain in 1901, representations of the Australian desert changed abruptly to express the new national optimism. It was now a challenge for ingenuity and technology: artesian water would transform it into rich agricultural and pastoral land. From its first appearance in films of the 1940s, it has continued to provide a stark, spectacular setting for celebrating the heroic virtues of Australians in the outback. *The Overlanders* (1946) was based on an actual cattle drive over 2,400 barren km from Western Australia to Queensland, undertaken to remove this food source from potential Japanese invaders and supply it to Australian troops. The intrinsic dangers of desert travel – starvation and thirst – are increased by a crocodile-infested river and a stampede. Similar elements contribute to Baz Luhrmann's epic film *Australia* (2008), which similarly features the droving of 1,500 head of cattle through the desert to Darwin for sale to the army at the time of the Japanese air-raids. The 'Aussie battlers' who wrested a precarious livelihood here exemplified true 'mateship', that most Australian of qualities, comprising equality, loyalty and friendship, stoicism expressed in wry humour and a wilful rebelliousness in the face of authority. Historian C.E.W. Bean wrote in 1911 of 'the mysterious half-desert country where men have to live the lives of strong men'.[16] Characters like the mailman on the Oodnadatta Track through the Simpson Desert and the elderly Daisy Bates, camped in the desert to minister to the Aborigines, supplanted explorers as national heroes and were embraced as idealized role models even by urban Australians.

In Antarctica, nationalism was most apparent in the race to the South Pole, seen as a demonstration of racial superiority. Since then, despite the Antarctic Treaty, competition in various forms continues in a continent already divided into a pie-chart of claims. Popularly known as the 'last wilderness', its significance is as much conceptual as physical: a frontier which we want both to conquer and to retain as pristine.

In Antarctica, too, explorers remain a major focus for mainstream writers. The figure of Scott, the problematic hero who was only runner-up in the race to the Pole, and whose whole party died on the return journey, offers fertile ground for probing motivation, the psychic journey and the symbolic parallels with every man's journey to self-knowledge. Scott's final expedition dominated thinking and writing about Antarctica, either directly, as in Douglas Stewart's verse play *Fire on the Snow* (1944), or thinly disguised as fiction, as in Thomas Keneally's novels *The Survivor* (1969) and *A Victim of the Aurora* (1977). In such writing it is Antarctica that *makes* heroes but paradoxically it has no identity without them. All these treatments of the explorers exploit tragic irony: the reader knows the outcome; the characters that struggle desperately on do not.

Here, as elsewhere, the desert is a highly gendered space. Women are absent, hardly even referred to. This, too, is part of desert mythology: that women could not endure such privation and must be protected from nature and bandits alike. Women scientists in Antarctica are increasing in numbers but some maintain they are still marginalized.[17] Ursula Le Guin's short story 'Sur' (1982) is a witty feminist critique of European-dominated history of conquest and obsession with being first. In her fantasy a group of South American women reaches the Pole two years ahead of Amundsen. Their success is due largely to their careful preparations, good housekeeping and amiable relations with each other, but they suppress their achievement because their purpose is only 'to go, to see. No more, no less', and because, as the narrator announces, 'we had left no sign there, for some man longing to be first might come some day, and find it, and know then what a fool he had been, and break his heart.'[18]

Gothic Horror

Traditionally associated with gratuitous cruelty, superstition and imprisonment in ancestral mansions, the term 'Gothic' might seem at first unrelated to the open spaces of the desert. Yet there are strong and insistent parallels between desert spaces and the Gothic in modern psychodramas where the desert represents the mindscape of horror within. Isolation through distance is no less absolute or terrifying than imprisonment by walls; heat, thirst and desolation are no less despotic than an aristocratic tyrant. The arbitrary terrors of the Gothic take physical form in violent, unpredictable sandstorms able to obliterate all geographical markers in minutes; the apparition of ghostly forms is parodied in mirages; and the eeriness, silence and loneliness of the desert elicit a more subtle sense of the supernatural. A post-Freudian reading of the Gothic as a trope for suppressed, psychological fears of imprisonment finds a reflection in the characteristics of the desert. Its indeterminate spaces of darkness and nothingness parallel the culturally repressed dread of alienation, of an inner void, and insist on dimensions of immensity and eternity that terrify the soul.

The Australian deserts were haunted for a century by the disappearance or death of the explorers, as grimly expressed by ballad writer Barcroft Boake (1866–1892):

> Where brown Summer and Death have mated –
> That's where the dead men lie! . . .
> Out where the grinning skulls bleach whitely
> Under the saltbush sparkling brightly;
> Out where the wild dogs chorus nightly –
> That's where the dead men lie![19]

As if natural dangers were not sufficient, the Australian desert has frequently been employed by film-makers as a location for horror and madness. In George Miller's *Mad Max* trilogy the desert provides the setting for a world after a nuclear holocaust, where there are no rules or protection in the battle for survival. Yet this desert of desperation also functions as parody. Stereotypes are satirized and fantastic narratives are played out across it by the lone warrior anti-hero Max, who defies cultural norms and time frames. In this Darwinian struggle, 'law' and punishment are determined by a wheel of fortune (the chance events of evolution); gangs murder for precious fuel to drive the national obsession, the car; and humans revert to primitive, ancestral types. The elevation of Max to hero status in the lost children's nightly 'tell' as the man who saved them mocks the reliance on legendary heroes to provide a national identity. The *Mad Max* films – *Mad Max* (1979), *Mad Max 2* (1981) and *Mad Max Beyond Thunderdome* (1985) – can thus be seen as bizarre, post-apocalyptic westerns where beaten-up vehicles have replaced horses and the quest is for fuel, not gold; where double-crossing is alive and well, but there is no sheriff to enforce order at the end.

One of the most macabre horror films set in the Australian desert is Greg McLean's *Wolf Creek* (2005), whose plot closely follows actual events that occurred in the Northern Territory in 2001.[20] It has elements of the road movie as three tourists, two

Poster of Mad Max, Aunty Entity and the lost children in *Mad Max Beyond Thunderdome* (dir. George Miller and George Ogilvie, 1985); original theatre poster by Richard Amsel.

young women and a man, set out to cross the continent from west to east. Having detoured to Wolf Creek in Western Australia to explore the impact crater formed by a 50,000-tonne meteorite, they discover their car will not start. They are 'found' by an outback character, Mick, who offers to tow them to his place and fix their car. Mick, however, is a killer. He tortures and kills the women; the man escapes but is initially disbelieved and the women's bodies are never found. In such a vast, remote desert region a killer maniac can easily escape detection.

By contrast with the political battles that have raged across the world's hot deserts, Antarctica exists in the world's imagination as untroubled by political contests, a *terra communis* for cooperative scientific research, where plankton and penguins inhabit a benign ecosystem. Fiction writers, however, have nearly always chosen to present it as a place of turmoil, even terror.

In Edgar Allan Poe's Gothic tale *The Narrative of Arthur Gordon Pym of Nantucket* (1837) and in his short story 'MS. Found

in a Bottle' (1833) the protagonists' ships are swept towards the South Pole. Pym plunges into a world of supernatural horror with 'ramparts of ice . . . like the walls of the universe' until a towering cataract of fog parts and draws the ship in, as a huge shrouded white figure appears. There the novel abruptly ends. The short story has a similar plot. The narrator's ship is hit by a Simoon in which only the narrator and a companion survive.[21] Driven south by the Simoon, the ship collides with a huge black galleon, which the narrator boards as it too heads south, approaching Antarctica. Eventually the ship enters a clearing in the ice but, caught in a huge whirlpool, it sinks. Only the narrator's manuscript of his adventures, which he had cast into the sea in a bottle, survives. Both these abrupt and enigmatic endings playfully suggest the ill-defined boundary between fact and fiction, reality and the supernatural. Poe's descriptions of life on board ship are realistic, yet the ghostly elements and the compulsion which drives the ships south to their mysterious and catastrophic ends seem more aligned to the supernatural: 'The Rime of the Ancient Mariner' without the gift of grace.

Wolfe Creek Crater, Western Australia.

Science fiction writers have also exploited Antarctica – as a terrestrial counterpart of space. It is almost as difficult to access as space, and those who go there experience isolation, hostile humans prepared to murder to acquire the treasures that the continent has to offer – plutonium, uranium, gold and oil – and even invasion from aliens. J. W. Campbell's science fiction horror story 'Who Goes There?' (1938) and two of the three films based on it, all titled *The Thing*,[22] engage with the recurrent ethical dilemma of science: how much is it safe to know? An Antarctic expedition unearths an alien spacecraft with frozen creatures in it, and the scientists deliberate whether to thaw, ignore or destroy them. Finally they liberate one specimen, the Thing, which immediately infiltrates the dogs and humans at the research station, mimicking them until they are indistinguishable from the originals. The isolation of Antarctica serves an essential plot function here, cutting off the group from help yet ultimately containing the menace. Its blizzards and white-outs also symbolize the shape-changing and hidden identity of the Thing.

The vastness and remoteness of Antarctica, where research bases may be over 1,000 km apart, also hide illicit activities and violence. In the thriller *Ice Station* (1999) Matthew Reilly rapidly demolishes the myth of a peaceful and altruistic scientific community. Treachery, scientific espionage and carnage created by hired military assassins are matched only by the natural violence of a killer whale pod emerging at the base of Wilkes Ice Station. In Antarctica humans are no longer at the top of the food chain. Similarly, the murder mystery film *Whiteout* (2009) involves scientists, multiple murders and uncut diamonds, while in David Smith's political eco-thriller *Freeze Frame* (1992) an undercover uranium mine near a French Antarctic base precipitates an assassination attempt and nations plotting mineral exploitation sabotage CRAMRA, the Convention on the Regulation of Antarctic Mineral Resource Activities.

Science fiction has also appropriated hot deserts to symbolize extreme extra-terrestrial environments that in turn parody Earth. Frank Herbert's novel *Dune* (1965, filmed by David

Lynch in 1985) is set on a desert planet that closely resembles Earth in its mechanisms for conserving water and especially in its reliance on, even addiction to, a spice that comes from the desert – a metaphor for oil. In the military science fiction film *Stargate* (1994), an ancient ring device unearthed in the Sahara opens a wormhole, enabling space-time travel to other stargates elsewhere in the universe – in this case a civilization closely resembling ancient Egypt. In all these examples the extreme conditions of the known desert provide a bridge for our imagination to envisage an unknown one where even more devastating events occur.

The Sense of Infinity

One of the first modern writers to associate the desert with infinity was the French *fin de siècle* novelist Pierre Loti,[23] best known for his romantic adventures and exotic travel writing. In 1894 he embarked on a journey to the Holy Land with a view to recovering some remnants of his religious faith. Although he failed to achieve this goal, he published an effervescent three-volume account of his expedition. The first volume, *The Desert* (1895), records a two-month pilgrimage from Suez to Gaza via Mount Sinai, the Arabian deserts and Jebel el-Tih, the Old Testament 'wilderness'. Loti observes the silence, the immensity and the permanence of these desert spaces.

> you get drunk on light and space . . . you know the heady
> intoxication of just being able to breathe, just being alive.
> You stretch your ears into the silence and you hear nothing,
> not a birdsong, nor the buzz of a fly, because there is nothing
> alive anywhere.
> . . . New spaces unfold on all sides; this tangible sign
> of their immensity increases our understanding of what
> wilderness is, but it also intimidates us more . . . One has
> the illusion of truly being united with universal permanence
> and time.[24]

Deserts also function as the external landscape for an inner spiritual journey. In 1910 Elliot Lovegood Grant Watson, an English biologist, spent six months alone in the Western Australian desert before joining the Radcliffe-Brown anthropological expedition to study Aboriginal culture in northwestern Australia. This powerful experience of desert solitude gave rise to six novels about the elemental mystical struggle between the rival powers of Western civilization and nature (epitomized by the desert) for possession of the European mind. In the novels *Desert Horizon* (1923) and *Daimon* (1925) the two central characters respond to the desert alternately with fascination and horror, re-enacting Watson's own struggle. The immensity and void so appalling to European settlers are, to Watson, positive qualities, prompting renunciation of material possessions as a prelude to spiritual enlightenment and 'some mystical affinity' with place.[25]

Randolph Stow's novel *Tourmaline* (1963), set in a fictional Western Australian desert town, opens with a hypnotic description associating the desert with age, immensity and barrenness:

> There is no stretch of earth more ancient than this. And so it is blunt and red and barren, littered with the fragments of broken mountains, flat, waterless. Spinifex grows here, but sere and yellow, and trees are rare, hardly to be called trees, some kind of myall with leaves starved to needles that fans out from the root and gives no shade.[26]

Stow was strongly influenced by the Tao Te Ching, the key text of Taoism, and in *Tourmaline* the physical landscape, continually threatened with extinction by the desert dust, symbolizes the endless transformation of things. The powerful closing description of a dust storm that obliterates every external marker of Tourmaline, as well as the narrator's sense of identity, in insubstantiality and flux, enacts this central tenet of Taoism – 'the land and the Tao are one'.[27] Words and phrases flow and repeat themselves like the flux of things.

Everything was flowing, insubstantial. The obelisk and the
hotel would appear through the dust and then, in an instant,
melt away . . .

It was like swimming under water, in a flooding river.
Dust sifted into my lungs; I was drowning . . . There was
nothing. Only myself swimming through the red flood that
had covered the world . . . What could this be if not the end
of the world?[28]

Powerful as *Tourmaline* is, it was Patrick White's novel *Voss*
(1957) that transformed the Australian desert into a dramatic
arena for psychological struggle, spiritual quest and final revelation. The development of White's protagonist Johann Ulrich
Voss, partly modelled on the nineteenth-century desert explorers Ludwig Leichhardt and Edward John Eyre,[29] is indicated
by his changed attitude: in the course of the novel he moves
from imposing his physical and intellectual conquest of the
desert 'by implicit right' to reaching something akin to Aboriginal awareness of a spiritual dimension in the land. Laura
Trevelyan, who mentally and spiritually shares Voss's journey
in his absence, identifies the attraction of the desert for him as
an extension of self: 'You are so isolated. That is why you are
fascinated by the prospect of desert places, in which you will
find your own situation . . . exalted . . . Everything is for your-
self.'[30] But in his last moments, awaiting decapitation by a
disillusioned Aboriginal boy, Voss is finally 'humbled in the
dust, and accepts the principles Laura would have liked him
to accept'.[31]

The protagonists of these fictions, like the many desert
explorers and travellers considered previously, undertake not
only a physical adventure but an internal journey from a safe,
domestic world to one that, as Yi-Fu Tuan comments, is 'vast,
overpowering and indifferent', where loss of self – even if it
provides moments of ecstasy – means death. 'Explorers of desert
and ice may be said to be half in love with piercing beauty and
half in love with death.'[32] With similar insight, White has
Laura remark at the end of *Voss*, 'Knowledge was never a matter

of geography. Quite the reverse, it overflows all maps that exist. Perhaps true knowledge only comes from death by torture in the country of the mind.'[33]

David Roberts, *The Royal Tombs*, *Petra*, 1839, lithograph.

Jean-Léon Gerôme, *Oedipus*, or *General Bonaparte in Egypt*, 1867–8, oil on canvas.

8 Deserts in Western Art

These paintings don't look like Antarctica, because it's impossible,
but they do feel like it . . . There are no familiar landmarks in this
place, no trees or buildings or people, it's a fractal landscape where
patterns are repeated from the huge to tiny, with nothing to hint
at scale . . . you can see everything yet understand very little.
Christian Clare Robertson

The art of indigenous desert peoples was almost always religious,
depicting spirit beings or creative powers within the land; but
Western eyes were trained to see differently. Artists focussed on
the visual, material world, painting a vertical 'slice' of sky and
land with geographical features, material objects and people
grouped upon it, scaled according to the rules of perspective. This
convention of Western art since the Renaissance was inadequate
for depicting the 'absences' that characterize deserts. Their relative featurelessness and clear, dry air, which creates the illusion
that distant objects are near at hand, subvert the traditions of
perspective and landscape composition.

This chapter considers four regions – North Africa and
the Middle East, the North American deserts, Australia and
Antarctica – where Western artists struggled to engage with an
alien landscape and were forced not only to devise new techniques
but sometimes to adopt new ways of seeing.

Orientalism

Before the twentieth century 'desert' for Europeans meant either
North Africa or the Middle East, areas associated with ancient
and respected civilizations. These landscapes, so well supplied
with cultural features, did not constitute a severe artistic challenge. Iconic objects such as the pyramids and the Sphinx provided visual interest, creating a three-dimensional composition
from a flat landscape. Further, artists almost invariably included

either contemporary ethnic figures or characters from history or the Bible.

Reports of Burckhardt's travels to Petra in 1812, and to Mecca in 1814, prompted the Scottish painter David Roberts to capitalize on this interest. In 1838 he expended his entire savings on a visit to Egypt. Subsequently he and his party crossed the Sinai Desert by camel to the ancient monastery of St Catherine and thence continued via Aqaba and Petra to Jerusalem. Roberts's sketches of Petra were the first images of this amazing city seen in the West and he had no hesitation in sacrificing accuracy for effect, removing a rock face to display the royal tombs or skewing a mountain to outline the monastery against the sky. His extensive portfolio of drawings was published as lithographs to great acclaim and with considerable profit. These images conveyed for the first time the indescribable barrenness of this mountainous area. His *View of Mt Sinai* (1839) shows his caravan in the foreground before the sharp peaks of the mountains, while his images of St Catherine's Monastery emphasize its extreme isolation. Since it has no door, it can be entered only through an opening 9 m up by means of a basket on a rope.

Napoleon's military campaign in Egypt (1798–1801) evolved into a scientific and cultural expedition, initiating a fashion for Orientalism. The spoils of his enterprises excited wonder in museums and inspired architects to replicate obelisks, Egyptian columns and Sphinx-like decorations. Artistic depictions of Egypt, notably by the French artists Jean-Léon Gerôme, Eugène Delacroix and Théodore Géricault, proliferated. Gerôme's *Oedipus*, or *General Bonaparte in Egypt* (1867–8), which shows Napoleon alone on his horse confronting the Sphinx in a desert waste, both exalts the Emperor and subtly suggests the vastness lying beyond imperial control.

European artists who visited Egypt and Morocco were struck by the brilliant light and intense colours. Street scenes depicting Arabs, pyramids and sphinxes, and historical paintings featuring heroic figures from Sardanapalus to Cleopatra, were popular subjects, as was the Bible. In their zeal to produce authentic biblical scenes, artists began to include the Middle East and

James Tissot, *The Magi Journeying*, 1886–94, oil on canvas.

Egypt in their Grand Tours. The French artist James Tissot, following his religious conversion, travelled to Egypt and Palestine to ensure the accuracy of his biblical scenes, which had previously been represented with European landscapes and costumes. His 350 watercolours of 'The Life of Christ', exhibited in the Paris Salon in 1894 during the first years of the French Catholic Revival, caused a sensation and an outpouring of reverence. They were published in the lavishly illustrated Tissot Bible (1896) and bought by the Brooklyn Museum in 1900. In *The Magi Journeying* (1886–94), which typifies Tissot's combination of authenticity and drama, three gold-robed figures mounted on camels ride across stony ground straight toward the viewer, followed by a retinue of camels and men weaving through a defile between barren, straw-coloured hills.

Other artists were inspired by the mystery and symbolism of the desert. *The Questioner of the Sphinx* (1863) by the American Elihu Vedder shows a kneeling Egyptian with his ear pressed to the mouth of the Giza Sphinx, awaiting answers, while tangible mysteries – a skull and ancient broken columns – lie scattered across the landscape. Gustave Achille Guillaumet's *Evening Prayer in the Sahara* (1863) depicts a group of Bedouin kneeling in prayer outside their black tents, but his later work *The Sahara* (1867) rejects such simple realism. Over the flat horizon a mirage-like group of men on camels, barely distinguishable through the heat haze, rides towards the carcass of a dead camel in the foreground, implicitly posing the question of whether such an end is inevitable in the desert.

The English artist William Holman Hunt, one of the Pre-Raphaelite Brotherhood, also chose to explore nature in relation to religious themes. For his symbolic work *The Scapegoat* (1854–8) he sat for weeks by the Dead Sea with a tethered goat brought from England, a brush in one hand and a gun in the other to deter attacks by Arabs.[1] Rotting plants and animal bones litter the foreground – elements of realism that outraged reviewers, who regarded the allegorical composition, especially the hapless goat, as demeaning Christ's sacrifice. Overall, Palestine proved a disappointment to European artists and writers. 'Physically Jerusalem

Elihu Vedder, *The Questioner of the Sphinx*, 1863, oil on canvas.

William Holman Hunt,
The Scapegoat, 1854–6,
oil on canvas.

is the foulest and odiousest [*sic*] place on earth ... horrid dreams
of squalor and filth, clamour and uneasiness, hatred and malice
and all uncharitableness', wrote Edward Lear.[2] Biblical artists
turned instead to Old Testament episodes set in Egypt that
allowed for splendour, drama and the latest archaeological finds.

The desert per se was rarely the focus of these pictures; rather,
it provided the background for some other source of interest,
whether architectural or narrative. Artists concentrated on local
figures, scenes from the Bible or monuments, bypassing the
crucial experience of spatial desolation. An empty desert was
deemed unpaintable within Western landscape conventions. With
the development of modernism in the twentieth century, new
modes of 'seeing' became available, but by that time artists had
tired of Egypt and Palestine and, with the exception of a small
number of war artists such as the Australian George Lambert,[3]
they saw no reason to resurrect them.

The American Desert

North American artists did not engage with the desert until
the Mexican War ended in 1848 and a surveying team was sent
to redefine the border. Accompanying them was the artist Henry
Cheever Pratt. His panoramic oil painting *View from Maricopa
Mountain near Rio Gila* (1855) adheres to rules of perspective,

with distant mountains and an expanse of the middle distance, but boldly confronts us in the foreground with the top part of a huge saguaro cactus in bloom. An arrow hangs down from the cactus, referencing a popular target sport of local Native Americans, unobtrusively present in the middle distance. The painting at first elicited surprise, almost disbelief, that such immense succulents could survive in desert country,[4] but it was gradually subsumed into the nationalistic framework of America's 'manifest destiny' as the inheritor of majestic landscapes, boundless plains and towering plants.

From the early 1900s until the 1950s hundreds of artists moved into the Californian desert to paint dunes and cholla, the cylindrical cactus native to the area. James ('Jimmy') Swinnerton began travelling through the southwestern states in the 1920s, painting desert landscapes in California, Arizona and New Mexico. He captured the dry wasteland of the four great North American deserts, lonely and desolate, their monumental buttes under vast skies imbued with allure and mystery. Swinnerton's contemporary Conrad Buff viewed the landscape of Zion National Park through the lens of modernism and with brilliant colours and sweeping brush strokes created geometrical, cubist blocks of colour.

America's most renowned desert artist, however, was Georgia O'Keeffe. Having made annual painting trips to New Mexico

Henry Cheever Pratt, *View from Maricopa Mountain Near the Rio Gila*, 1855, oil on canvas.

since 1929, she finally moved there permanently in 1949, drawn by the convoluted desert mountains. 'It was the shapes of the hills there that fascinated me. The reddish sand hills with the dark mesas behind them.'[5] The clear, dry desert air erased the sense of distance so that remote hills gave the illusion of appearing close while remaining distant. O'Keeffe expressed this paradox in the succession of receding layers which we must traverse visually through alternating light and dark bands, as in *Near Abiquiu, New Mexico* (1930). O'Keeffe was also intrigued by the dead animal bones lying in the desert and seeming an integral part of it. She wrote:

> To me they are as beautiful as anything I know. To me they are strangely more living than the animals walking around ... [they] cut sharply to the center of something that is keenly alive on the desert even tho' it is vast and empty and untouchable – and knows no kindness with all its beauty.[6]

Earlier in her career O'Keeffe had produced large-format close-ups of flowers painted in microscopic detail. Paradoxically, she used a similar technique to represent vastness in her desert landscapes. A single element, whether bones or mountains, is observed in great detail and enlarged to fill the frame without reference to context, as in *Ram's Head, White Hollyhock and Little Hills* (1935), and abstract, stylistic works such as *Black Mesa Landscape, New Mexico/Out Back of Marie's II* (1930),[7] which convey the material solidity and immensity of the desert with a majestic, even transcendental quality.

Photography provided a new perspective on deserts in terms of both colour and structure. With colour photography, popularized through the *National Geographic Magazine* from its inception in 1888, the rich red of the desert exploded into life for those who had previously seen only absence of vegetation. Equally influential in North American cultural history were Ansel Adams's black-and-white photographs of the Nevada desert, the Grand Canyon, Death Valley and Yosemite National Park. His high-resolution photos, conveying both immensity

Georgia O'Keeffe,
*Ram's Head, White
Hollyhock and Little
Hills*, 1935, oil on
canvas.

and minute detail, became icons of America's national identity. Although they appear natural at first, Adams's images were not actually realistic but made use of contrived perspectives and lighting to generate what he termed the 'spiritual-emotional aspects' of the Sublime. This emotive response was often stronger than any actual experience of place, powerfully influencing how people subsequently 'saw' such scenes. Lamenting the loss of wilderness and opportunities for solitude, Adams used his images to promote the environmental goals of the Sierra Club, founded by John Muir in 1892 to preserve wild places. He became a charismatic figure in the wilderness movement, a prophetic voice calling for the creation of national parks and protection of wild areas, notably deserts, from developmental projects. His photos remain in circulation in books and calendars, promoting his philosophy that we can live in harmony with nature without destroying it.

Australian Deserts

Because of the inaccessibility of the Central Australian deserts, the first Europeans to encounter them were explorers and artist-surveyors, who attempted to apply techniques of topo-graphical drawing to a flat and featureless landscape. Their frustration is eloquently depicted in Edward Frome's watercolour *First View of the Salt Desert – Called Lake Torrens* (1843)[8] and the irony of the word 'called' in his title. Frome, Surveyor-General of South Australia, here depicts either himself or his assistant inspecting a monotonous scene in which the figure provides the sole interest. The level telescope through which he searches vainly for some geographical feature emphasizes the flatness of the country. The desolation of this painting is imputed to nature's deception – a 'lake' that is only a salt desert – but its emotional dejection arises from something outside its frame: the frustrated hopes of the colonists.

The first professional artist included in an exploring expedition was Ludwig Becker, a member of Burke and Wills's ill-fated party that in 1860 set out to cross the continent from south to north. Becker, a naturalist as well as an artist, produced meticulous scientific drawings of desert plants and animals and superbly evocative watercolours of the landscape. An admirer of Caspar David Friedrich, he was the first artist to see here an antipodean equivalent of the Romantic Sublime. One of his boldest compositions was the sketch *Crossing the Terrick-Terrick Plains, August 29, 1860* (1860), showing two diverging lines of men emerging from an invisible central point beyond the horizon. Those on the left are mounted on camels; on the right are horse riders and covered wagons. Between them rides Burke on his prancing horse, Billy. The line of camels proceeds towards the skeleton of a cow, seemingly in premonition of the expedition's disastrous outcome, though Becker could not have known this. Both riders and mounts have a translucent look owing to the shimmering heat rising from the plains; with hindsight, this imparts a ghostly quality and dramatic irony to the scene of the doomed expedition.

The mirages that deceived and frustrated his companions symbolized for Becker a reality beyond corporeal experience. In *Border of the Mud-Desert near Desolation Camp* he plays with Fata Morgana effects to make us, too, doubt what we see. The dingoes and emus and the mud cracking and curling seem to reassure us

that the scene is real, yet the ephemeral appearance of the camel riders emerging from the glare associates them rather with the illusory lake and trees in the distance. The depiction of the mid-day glare suggests the possible influence of J.M.W. Turner, as well as Becker's own fascination with representing light.

Ludwig Becker, *Border of the Mud-Desert Near Desolation Camp*, 1861, watercolour on paper.

Systematically bullied by the expedition leader Burke, plagued by heat and flies and suffering the exhausting conditions of the expedition and the lack of adequate art materials, Becker nevertheless improvised means to render his delicate, translucent landscapes. Substituting eucalyptus gum for gum arabic, he created a surface he could finely cross-hatch with Indian ink to indicate shadows, or coat with clear washes or varnish to suggest transparency. These intriguing watercolours remain the most enduring and significant outcome of this ill-advised, ill-fated undertaking.

The next breakthrough in depicting desert came via a very urban art movement, modernism, which emphasized clear, sharp lines, geometric forms and flat blocks of colour. The first artist to make a connection between modernism and the Australian desert was Hans Heysen, whose earlier, very successful career had been based on his evocative paintings of eucalypts, regarded as symbols of nationalism. In 1926 Heysen visited the arid Flinders Ranges of South Australia where he was astonished at the clarity of vision resulting from the dry air, the sharply outlined hills and rocks that seemed closer than in reality, and the monotone, geometrical shapes of a landscape almost bereft of foliage. He wrote to a fellow artist:

> My first impression upon arrival was that of expanse, of simplicity and beauty of contours – the light flat and all objects sharply defined; distances very deceptive, and no appreciable atmospheric difference between the foreground and the middle distances ... scale becomes an important relative factor.[9]

The immense size of the rock formations and features he wished to depict forced Heysen to locate them in the distance in his paintings, necessarily simplifying their forms and accentuating their shapes. Fascinated by the seemingly contemporary art forms that resulted, he wrote, 'There are scenes ready made, which seem to say, "here is the very thing you moderns are trying to paint". Fine, big, simple forms against clear transparent skies – & a sense of spaciousness everywhere.'[10] Heysen was especially captivated by the massive sandstone monoliths and fractured slabs of rock, which he painted exclusively in drought, as in *Guardian of the Brachina Gorge* (1937).[11] Indeed, when he visited the area after rain and found new grass springing up, he refused to paint it, finding it 'most disconcerting and out of harmony'.[12]

Australian stamps issued in 1985 reproducing Sidney Nolan, *Musgrave Ranges* (1949), and Russell Drysdale, *The Walls of China* (1945).

Further revisioning of the desert was supplied by Russell Drysdale, who confronted head on the technical problems of representing a flat, empty land and a featureless sky. His monochromatic palette of browns, yellows and ox-blood skies, as in *The Walls of China (Gol Gol)* (1945),[13] conveyed the sense of imprisonment produced by the oppressive unity of earth and sky. Severing any links with naturalism, he transformed the stark and barren landscapes into a Surrealist world peopled by misshapen, anorexic figures who claw an existence from this inhospitable land, yet contrive to express a jaunty attitude to their minimal existence.

In *Man Feeding His Dogs* (1941)[14] the desolation of this landscape, with its spindly, dead tree trunks, a broken cartwheel and an abandoned chair hanging from a branch, is countered by the elegant greyhounds leaping joyfully to receive their food. Drysdale's desert landscapes are often disfigured by discarded rubbish from settlers now departed. Junk iron, broken windmills, rusting tins and pipes provide surreal and parodic statuary, mimicking the outlines of emus in the middle distance.

Heysen had revolutionized shapes and Drysdale colours, but the most radical change in depicting the Australian desert came with air travel, which allowed artists to see at a glance the immensity and physiognomy of the vast, inaccessible areas that had defeated the early explorers. While this distancing empowers the viewer, it reduces the land to contours and ultimately to abstract patterns. The first artist to paint the Australian desert from the air was Sidney Nolan. Flying over the Musgrave Ranges out to Ayers Rock (now Uluru) in 1949, 'he was both tremendously excited and repelled by the wind, desolation and phenomenal light.'[15] From this aerial perspective, the antique, red hills, like volcanic craters, march endlessly into the distance, creating the illusion that the whole continent is laid out like a relief map vast enough to show the curve of the Earth's surface. By juxtaposing colour and deep shadow Nolan contrived to give a deceptive impression of detailed topography. The fast-drying Ripolin enamel he used gave a startling shine to the scene, indicating the brilliance of the light and the glow of heat.

Nolan's desert landscapes show an uninhabitable land that he himself called

> cruel . . . harsh and barren beyond any other part of the habitable globe. For thousands of miles one sees nothing but red desert, the bones of a few dead animals, and occasionally the sordid remains of a street where somebody looking for gold had tried to build a township.[16]

Yet despite their emotional detachment, these paintings engage with a conceptual issue. Nolan later remarked, 'I wanted to deal ironically with the cliché of the "dead heart" . . . I wanted to paint the great purity and implacability of the landscape.'[17] More than any other artist, Nolan developed a new myth of the Australian landscape that was both individual and universal, topical and timeless.

Nolan was also fascinated by the figures of the explorers Burke and Wills. Seeing from the air the barren terrain they crossed, he felt enormous respect for their determination; yet, rejecting the heroic imagery of nineteenth-century art, he shows them stiff and insecure in a deserted landscape, archetypal representatives of Europeans unable to adjust to this alien continent.[18] The art critic Barrett Reid remarked:

> Nolan's vision is a tragic one. It is mocking . . . it is cruel . . . and it occupies a vast and arid inner space as lonely as the surface of the moon . . . It is the silence after Auschwitz. It is a central fact of contemporary experience, which we cannot avoid.[19]

Antarctica

Despite their immense differences, Antarctica and Australia have presented artists with similar problems. An ice desert is even more bereft of features than its Central Australian counterpart, and the challenge of depicting emptiness, unrelieved whiteness and space without perspective daunted artists from the first encounter. As the historian Stephen Pyne remarks, 'The very simplicity of Antarctica made it alien . . . the interior icescape could not be made to look like any familiar landscape . . . [it was] abstract, minimal, conceptual.'[20] Antarctica's landscape makes its impact through negatives – through what is *not* there, rather than what is.

For the topographical artists of the eighteenth-century sea voyages, Antarctica's shoreline appeared only as a barren, white expanse. Far more interesting visually were the fantastic shapes and colours of floating icebergs. William Hodges, the artist on Cook's second Pacific voyage, produced one of the first widely publicized images of Antarctica, *The Ice Islands, seen the 9th of Janry. 1773.*[21] The picture is full of movement. A mountainous iceberg rears up on the right, while in the centre foreground a party of sailors in a rowing boat hacks at a smaller berg to obtain ice for water supplies. In another boat a man, presumably the ship's naturalist Johann Reinhold Forster or his son Georg, aims his gun at wheeling sea birds for food or specimens. Cook's ship *Resolution* rides majestically at anchor in the middle distance. It is an elegant, aesthetic composition, indicating the grandeur of the icebergs but bypassing the artistic difficulties presented by the ice shelf.

More emotionally evocative were the wholly imaginative illustrations by Gustave Doré for Coleridge's *The Rime of the Ancient Mariner* (1878). In Plate 6, 'The Ice was All Around', Doré presents a ghostly ship with gleaming icicles dripping from its spars (see page 150). Appropriately to the Gothic tone of the poem, the ship appears totally imprisoned by icebergs, 'mast-high', above which a moon rainbow forms a curved bridge across the walls of ice and the albatross hovers benignly over the ship.

As in Australia, artists were permitted to accompany expeditions to the interior of the Antarctica only in order to illustrate

William Hodges, 'The Ice Islands, seen the 9th of Janry. 1773', from James Cook's *A Voyage towards the South Pole...* (1777).

the explorers' published accounts, the profits from which were important in recouping the debts incurred. These scientific reports were either inimical to illustration (being concerned with wind, temperature or seismic measurements), or related to the animal species available for study. Artists were left to depict expedition members heroically battling the elements or celestial events. It was not considered important, or even possible, to illustrate the landscape.

Artists on Antarctic expeditions were also plagued by logistical difficulties. Paints and fingers freeze in these temperatures, so they were forced to use chalks or make pencil sketches with annotated notes of the colours to be used in producing a subsequent watercolour. Photographers of the heroic age suffered even worse adversity. Their equipment, weighing up to 100 kg, required extra sledges, usually man-hauled, while howling gales and frequent blizzards destabilized mounted cameras and reduced visibility to zero. The equipment surrounding Louis Bernacchi and his dog Joe in Stephen Walker's bronze statue on the Hobart waterfront is a faithful representation of an Antarctic photographer's gear.[22] On sunny days the glare off the ice was blinding and the dry air annihilated perspective. Hence the majority of photographs from this 'heroic' period focussed on the ships, the huts or the men. Icebergs, especially those with fantastic shapes, were considered photogenic and Herbert Ponting, a member of Scott's expedition of 1910–13, employed an ice cave as a frame with posed expeditioners as human interest; but in general ice per se was not regarded as a possible subject for art. Frank Hurley, who accompanied Mawson's and Shackleton's expeditions, produced some spectacular images, most famously that of Shackleton's ship *Endurance* trapped in pack ice. To make this image Hurley placed remotely triggered flares on the masts and spars of the ship and along its hull, effectively converting it into a giant flashcube in the darkness of the polar night.

Possibly the most remarkable paintings of the 'heroic age' were the delicate watercolours of Edward Wilson, doctor and naturalist on Scott's expeditions. His illustrations of natural phenomena were both scientifically accurate and artistically conceived,

James Francis Hurley,
'Endurance' in the Ice,
1915, gelatin dry plate.

showing his fascination with celestial occurrences – aurora,
parhelia and paraselenae. His elegant composition of Scott's ship
Discovery from the first expedition, with penguins jumping off
an ice shelf in the foreground, parhelia encircling the rigging
and sea birds wheeling around the ship, is based on meticulous
observation, as indicated by his field sketch of parhelia over the
Ross Ice Shelf, made en route to the South Pole. The colours
and brightness of the parhelia rings are described beside his
sketch in words, which Wilson would have referred to to complete
the watercolour, had he survived the journey. Like Turner, one of
his artistic heroes, Wilson was fascinated with the challenge of

painting light under these conditions – light reflected from the frozen sea, steam clouds above Mt Erebus, auroral displays, parhelia, lunar halos, refracted images of mountains and mirages.

When Antarctic exploration recommenced after the Second World War the emphasis was still on reporting and documentation and the dominant artistic medium was photography, commissioned by publications including *National Geographic Magazine* and *Audubon Magazine* and, later, documentary films for television. There seemed to be little place for painters. However, in 1963, under the auspices of the United States, Sidney Nolan was flown into McMurdo Sound to make an artistic record of the continent. Nolan, who had transformed the Australian desert into a mythological stage on which to display the carcass of the continent and symbolic images of Burke and Wills, immediately identified parallels with Antarctica as another immense, barren space first seen from the air. Many of his Antarctic landscapes therefore have an implicit aerial perspective, evident in *Glacier* (2 September 1964). As in Central Australia, Nolan focusses on the geological skeleton of the land with its spine of ranges but here, instead of stasis, he presents a deep blue and green river of ice snaking between two ice mountains and seeming actually to move. The inter-continental parallels extend to his images of explorers. The *Explorer* (1964) with a hood of translucent ice and staring goggled eyes mimics an ice statue mocked by its frozen environment, just as Nolan's Australian explorers had appeared to be ridiculed by the desert.

Whereas the expedition artists had concentrated on celestial events, which provided colour and movement in a landscape seemingly bereft of these, modern artists have largely left these to scientific photographers and focussed on the ice itself. They are captivated by its refracted colours, its mutability, the immense variety of forms it can assume and the prospect of depicting these phenomena in ways that engage with the postmodern vision of a fractured reality. This artistic challenge has inspired new techniques in painting, photography, pastels and etchings.

During the 1970s the British artist David Smith spent twelve months in Antarctica. Fascinated by ice in all its stages and forms, he recorded its structure in paintings that are both representational and abstract patterns. *The Sea Freezing* (1975–6 or 1979–80), a study in blue, shows the first platelets of pancake ice forming on the surface of the sea. The pancakes are outlined in small white dots suggestive of the movement of the plates bumping together and the shimmering reflection from their edges, so that the sea appears to be in constant movement. Smith noted that ice, far from being colourless, reflected colour from every source and provided its own rainbow effects by refracting light from its many planes and angles. In *Low Sun and Icebergs* he depicts a scene saturated with the colours of sunset in almost shocking contrast to the blue tones we customarily associate with ice. These effects of light and ice would surely 'have entranced the great Impressionist painters'.[23] Smith, like Wilson, was also fascinated by celestial phenomena. His depiction of a paraselena at Halley Bay captures the diagrammatic symmetry of the event.

The Australian artist Christian Clare Robertson has explored more complex ways of representing the intricate structure of ice. Antarctica was part of her *Extreme Landforms* project, an artistic study of tectonic plate movement. Flying into Mawson, she saw it from the air as a fractured sea, like a piece of knitting, with slab-like bergs resting on it, or as a knife-edged ice wall plunging into a crevasse of shades of blue. Four of her works were chosen for reproduction on Antarctic Territory stamps. In *Twelve Lake* (1990), so named for the XII-shaped markings on the hills behind it, the cracking surface ice forms a three-dimensional grid like flexible metallic mesh and, because the water beneath is so clear and shallow, the cracks form a parallel intersecting pattern of shadows on the gravel bottom of the lake. Robertson continually plays with perspective to mimic the uncertainty of scale and distance induced by the clear air. *Ice Cave* (1990) introduces all the confusion of an M. C. Escher drawing to induce disorientation in the viewer. Are we inside the cave, or outside looking in? A narrow tunnel in brilliant blue, seemingly dissociated from the surrounding jumble of fractured ice, appears to veer vertically upwards at the end but its direction at any one point is in doubt.

David Smith, *The Sea Freezing*, 1975–6 or 1979–80, watercolour.

David Smith, *A Paraselena, Halley Bay*, Antarctica, 1975–6 or 1979–80, oil on canvas.

Lynne Andrews, *Ice Cliff of the Glacier Tongue*, 1997, oil on cotton duck, two panels.

Christian Clare Robertson, *Ice Cave*, 1990, oil on linen.

opposite: Christian Clare Robertson, *Twelve Lake*, 1990, oil on linen.

Another Australian artist visitor, Lynne Andrews, has also engaged with the challenge of representing aspects of ice. Her diptych *Ice Cliff of the Glacier Tongue* (1997) recreates the vertical immensity of the Campbell Glacier Tongue towering vertiginously above the viewer in a zodiac inflatable boat. Andrews writes of this composition:

> These cliffs represent the side of the glacier, which . . . harbours deep blue, vertical crevasses, small ice caves and sharp icicles. Some fissures reveal a brownish detritus . . . Ironically this ultra-solid ice mass will calve to form icebergs that will float off into the sea and eventually disintegrate. The medium of oil paint is appropriate to evoke the gleam of the ice and the process of oil painting mirrors the slow and gradual layering of the ice in the formation of a glacier.[24]

In their determination to record this frozen white world these contemporary artists were forced to abandon the fruitless attempt to coerce Antarctica into a formal landscape composition. Instead, they launched out into new modes of representation, new modes of seeing. Drawing on the insights of Impressionism, modernism and Cubism, they have produced images that oscillate teasingly between realistic observation and the subversion of expectation that this terrain induces. They see, as in poet Les Murray's words about the Australian desert:

> a field all foreground, and equally all background,
> like a painting of equality. Of infinite detailed extent
> like God's attention. Where nothing is diminished
>   by perspective.[25]

9 Exploitation and Opportunity

> Aside from random deposits of minerals, it [desert] is valuable
> mainly as a zone in which to shed the shackles of civilization . . .
> In the desert one is liberated from all restraint because nobody's
> around to notice. That's why we explode bombs there. Or dump
> things that might create problems elsewhere. They can't do any
> damage in the desert; there's nothing out there to damage.
> David Darlington, *The Mojave* (1996)

Darlington's words are heavily ironic. His next paragraph begins,
'Or so it was thought until rather recently . . . when a new view
was revealed to civilization: *the desert is beautiful!*' But, sadly, the
above quotation describes all too accurately what has happened,
and continues to happen, in many desert areas.

The year 2006 was declared the International Year of Deserts
and Desertification and a United Nations decision was taken to
control desertification and land degradation, which both involve
the spread of desert areas. Alerted to such risks, it is easy to think
that deserts are less in need of protection from us than we from
them. However, it is timely to recall that a similar mode of thinking was once applied to wilderness and rainforest: they grew so
fast that they could certainly regenerate themselves. How could
they need protection?

Desertification, the degradation of semi-arid drylands bordering true deserts, usually through human activity, should not be
confused with true deserts, which are formed quite differently.
'They are unique, highly adapted natural ecosystems, providing
life-supporting services on the planet and supporting human
populations in much the same way as other ecosystems.'[1] Because
they have evolved to survive water scarcity, drought in itself is not
a threat to deserts. But what they cannot easily survive is human-
induced degradation through overgrazing, deforestation, erosion,
unsustainable farming, irrigation-induced salinity, soil and water
contamination by agrochemicals or fracking, industrial-scale
mining and the traffic flow associated with these activities and with

tourism. Already some 20 per cent of the world's deserts are affected by land degradation,[2] and, because many of these threats are relatively new and sudden, deserts have not had time to adapt.

Until recently deserts were regarded as economically worthless, but increasingly they are recognized as treasure houses of wealth and opportunity. Many have underground assets of minerals, diamonds, uranium, coal, oil and gas. Above ground they offer 'empty space' for expansion of grazing and agriculture, urban spread, developing and testing nuclear weapons and generating solar power; they also have unique potential for scientific research in many areas and have become attractive destinations for tourism and leisure. These assets boost the economies of many formerly poor countries but there is almost always a cost levied on the environment, and usually also on the indigenous peoples who, while providing the major source of labour, are most often excluded from the profits.

Apart from human-induced degradation, there is damage to deserts from climate change, which affects the whole planet and threatens the biodiversity of established deserts. As we have seen, plants and animals have evolved particular adaptations that allow them to survive in these hostile environments but, faced with further increases in aridity at higher temperatures, they have no fall-back position and will become extinct. Currently endangered desert species include the sand gazelle, cheetah, white oryx, addax, Barbary sheep and Arabian tahr.[3]

Antarctica, dominated by its blanket of ice and snow and the surrounding Southern Ocean, is both sensitive to, and a major agent of, climate change. The balance between water storage as ice and its discharge as melt and the amount of CO_2 trapped in the ice are important factors in the global climate system, affecting greenhouse gas levels, rising sea levels, the acidification of the oceans, the rate of climate change and environmental mutability.

Expansion of grazing, settlement and agriculture not only lead to increased desertification by removing the vegetation cover but, in established deserts, interrupt plant and animal succession. Whereas in other terrains renewal of vegetation begins quickly after disturbance by fire or moderate clearing for roadways, in deserts, where there are no intermediate species to prepare the soil or shade the habitat, only the original, adapted plant forms can return. This may take years, even decades, or may never happen. Disturbances to desert ecosystems are multiplying rapidly as even formerly despised land becomes an attractive site for expansion. Roads and pipelines snake out into desert areas, bringing in their wake power plants, petrol stations, houses and towns, increasing erosion and burying the original desert beneath a new one, paved with concrete and indistinguishable from neighbouring cities.

For the impoverished inhabitants of desert regions, irrigation systems may seem an unmixed blessing, and in the short term they can convert aridity into productivity. But such transformation comes at a significant cost. Drainage of underground aquifers leads to soil poisoning through salinization. Beneath the central Australian deserts lies the Great Artesian Basin, one of the world's largest inland drainage areas, from which water rises to the surface at natural springs. Bores drilled to simulate these springs and access water for stock, agriculture and mining have significantly decreased the flow from the natural mound springs where fish, bird life and a rich ecosystem had formerly flourished. Elsewhere the effects have been far more catastrophic.

The Kyzyl Kum Desert is the site of one of the world's worst ecological disasters – the shrinking of the Aral Sea. This has been caused by extensive irrigation from the Amu Darya and the Syr Darya, the major rivers feeding this landlocked sea, to support Uzbekistan's cotton industry and rice and wheat crops in the desert.[4] Since the irrigation scheme began in 1960, the Aral Sea, once the fourth largest lake in the world, has shrunk to a mere 15 per cent of its former size, leaving in its wake vast salt plains. The remnant sea is now 2.4 times as salty as the oceans, killing many species of native fish and destroying the local fishing industry. In addition, it has become polluted with fertilizer and chemical pesticides that have been implicated in respiratory diseases and cancers. Dust storms blowing from the 40,000 square km of now-exposed lakebed contain dangerous agricultural chemicals, and salt-laden dust has settled on neighbouring fields, making them infertile.[5] Dismissing the southern Aral Sea as a hopeless case, the government of Kazakhstan partitioned it off with a dam to increase the level of the northern Aral Sea. This temporary 'solution' has only extended the Aral Karakum desert to the south, where deposits have been washed from the irrigated fields. Pollution has no respect for boundaries. Trace pesticide residues from this area have now been found in Greenland glaciers, Russian fields and the blood of Antarctic penguins.

The Karakum Desert itself has also been irrigated. The 1,375-kilometre Karakum Canal, begun in 1954, vastly increased productivity of the area but has led to severe salinization of the soil, producing a visible salt crust.

Desert areas with deposits of oil and gas have acquired a booming economy but the ecological losses may far outweigh the gains. Oil spills on land and in bodies of fresh water are frequent in North African and Arabian deserts. These affect surface resources and a wide range of subsurface organisms linked in a complex food chain that includes human food sources. Additionally, they can harm the environment by producing a lethal coating of oil on animals and plants, and by the toxicity of oil itself. In 1991, during the Gulf War, Iraqi forces destroyed 1,164 Kuwaiti oil wells, releasing 60 million barrels of oil into the desert and contaminating soil and ground water. They also released 11 million barrels of oil into the Persian Gulf, killing thousands of sea birds and severely damaging the aquatic ecosystem, including sea turtles, dugongs, dolphins, fish and shrimps. Oil fires, which could not be extinguished for nine months, poured pollution into the atmosphere. Tanks speeding across the desert damaged the top layer of soil, releasing unstable, rolling sand dunes. Far worse are the long-term effects of uranium munitions fired from low-flying American aircraft and the 300 tons of depleted uranium dropped during 1991 by the U.S. and NATO, which have contaminated soil and water.

These environmental disasters were deliberately caused during war, but near the Turkmenistan village of Derweze, in the middle of the Karakum Desert, disaster occurred by accident in 1971 when Soviet geologists, drilling for natural gas, bored into a cavern filled with gas. The ground beneath the cavern collapsed, leaving a

Derweze, the 'Door to Hell', Turkmenistan. Natural gas burns out of control from a crater caused by a mining collapse, 2010.

crater 70–100 m wide. To avoid the release of poisonous methane, it was decided to fire the gas. The fire has been burning ever since, releasing tonnes of carbon into the atmosphere. Local people call it 'the door to hell'.[6]

Although mining activities may directly affect only small areas, they have extended impact on surrounding areas. Modern mining methods are highly water-intensive and mining companies often excavate beneath the water table to pump and remove the groundwater in a practice known as 'dewatering'. This can cause springs and wells in the region to dry up and land to subside; it also threatens oases, wetlands and irrigation.

Further problems occur when a mine has exhausted its potential. Abandoned mining sites are a dumping ground for by-products and rubble, including highly toxic chemicals that percolate into the ground and the water table. Wind and flash floods spread these toxins further. Abandoned copper, lead, and nitrate mines in the Puna of Chile remain potential sources of contamination from chemical spillage.[7] High-altitude mines near the sources of rivers that provide irrigation systems and drinking water are particularly dangerous.

Mining of both metallic and non-metallic minerals such as phosphates and uranium is important to the economy of most Saharan countries, but this new wealth rarely benefits the indigenous peoples, since multinational companies import skilled workers and pay minimal wages to the unskilled labourers whose land has been appropriated. Much of the Namib is protected but some significant areas of biodiversity are at risk because of prospecting, copper mining and onshore and offshore diamond mining, on which Namibia's economy is heavily dependent.

Apart from natural resources that can be extracted, deserts offer 'empty space' that can be cordoned off for weapons research and nuclear testing. The u.s. Naval Air Weapons Station, 4,500 square km at China Lake on the western edge of the Mojave Desert, just 240 km northeast of Los Angeles, has been the site for development and testing of American airborne weapon systems since 1950,[8] and Lop Nur at the edge of the Taklamakan Desert has been a nuclear weapons test site since 1964. In Australia, between 1955 and 1963, the British government conducted nuclear tests at Maralinga and Emu Field in the Great Victoria Desert, leaving vast areas, including Aboriginal lands, contaminated with plutonium-239, uranium-235 and other radioactive materials.

Even activities that appear innocent and even beneficial to the overall health of the planet, such as solar power generation, are not without risk of causing short-term despoliation during their construction. Scientists engaged in research projects in sensitive desert areas have depleted resources, leaving waste and pollution in their wake. The scientific bases in Antarctica are now being 'cleaned up' and all waste is being returned to the countries concerned, but it has taken a century for such responsibility to develop.

Tourism is equally problematic. On the one hand it generates awareness and respect for desert places and their fragility; on the other it introduces large numbers of people, with their accustomed expectations of access to power, water, fresh food, transport and entertainment. Heavy foot traffic on sensitive soils can destroy fragile vegetation for decades, perhaps irrevocably; and the long-term consequences of trampled dunes, excessive off-track vehicle traffic damaging slow-growing vegetation and increasing wind and water erosion, particularly in wadi beds subject to periodic

flooding, are yet to be fully realized. Culturally the looting of
archaeological sites and the destruction of rock art are difficult to
monitor in remote areas and have been disturbingly frequent.

In Antarctica there have been unique moves to curtail such
potential damage. In 1959, at the very height of the Cold War,
nations with territorial claims to areas of Antarctica waived them
temporarily in the Antarctic Treaty, which outlined the future
research and management of the continent. Twelve nations signed
the Treaty at that time; today there are 44 signatories. Subsequently, in 1991, the Madrid Protocol extended the Antarctic
Treaty to prohibit mining before 2048 and, even then, only if two-
thirds of the signatories agreed. Currently, therefore, the most
invasive impact comes from tourists and those working at the
bases. The former are more numerous but stay only briefly and
tour companies are aware that their licences may be removed if
they disregard their environmental responsibilities. There remains
concern that scientific personnel pose the highest risk of introducing alien species into the ecosystem. Pathogens from domestic
chickens are infecting penguins, distemper from the former sledge
dogs has spread to seals, and albatrosses and petrels are threatened
by bacteria imported on clothing.[9] Bases are experimenting with
alternative energy resources to replace oil, and with water recycling; and whereas waste was once dumped into the sea or down
a crevasse, the Madrid Protocol requires all rubbish to be cleaned
up and, where possible, removed from the continent. Protected
areas are being set up, off-limits to vehicles, and the number of

visitors, including expeditioners, is strictly controlled. However, smaller expeditions are more difficult to monitor and there is no guarantee that derelict vehicles left by private expeditioners will be removed.

Inequitable access to land, human population dynamics and poverty in developing countries are some of the most significant factors that increase over-exploitation of deserts. The populations of countries with large areas of desert often face additional challenges, both political and social, from the competition for access to strategic water and soil. These situations generally result in unequal concentration of wealth and land resources, producing social unrest, uprisings and, inevitably, further land degradation. Possible solutions require a multi-disciplinary approach to reconciling the needs of local and global communities, accommodating humans within the broader ecosystem and generating respect for these unique and beautiful places.

Fortunately two properties of deserts – the solar radiation that falls on them and the arid atmosphere above them – are also being used for beneficial purposes with minimal impact on the

Artist's impression of the Atacama Large Millimeter/ submillimeter Array (ALMA) site on the Chajnantor plain, Atacama Desert, 5000 m above sea level in the Chilean Andes. ALMA is the largest ground-based astronomy project in existence and will comprise a giant array of 12-m submillimetre quality antennas, with baselines of several kilometres. The project is a collaboration between Europe, East Asia and North America in cooperation with the Republic of Chile, to be completed 2013.

environment. Desertec, a German-led project, is using an uninhabited area of the Sahara near Beni Suef in Egypt to erect 6,000 parabolic troughs with a combined surface area of 130,000 square m to generate solar power. This is only one-seventh of the power plant's eventual capacity. When completed it will provide electricity not only to the Middle East and North Africa but also to Europe, greatly decreasing the need for fossil fuels.[10]

Deserts also offer unparalleled research opportunities for one particular scientific discipline: astronomy. Cloudless nights, a dry atmosphere and minimal light pollution create ideal observing conditions. The European Southern Observatory (ESO) has built, and continues to build, some of the world's most advanced telescopes at three different high-altitude sites in Chile, taking advantage of the Atacama's hyper-aridity and its 340 or more clear nights per year. They include the New Technology Telescope (NTT) at La Silla, the Very Large Telescope (VLT) at Paranal and the Atacama Large Millimeter/submillimeter Array (ALMA) at Llano de Chajnantor. ALMA's 64 linked 12-m radio antennas will be used to study relic radiation of the Big Bang some 13 billion years ago, and the molecular gas and dust that are the building blocks of the universe. Radiation at sub-millimetre wavelengths is normally absorbed by water in the atmosphere, but this problem

The La Silla Observatory in the Atacama Desert, visible on the distant summit, is located in a semi-desert region 100 km north of the La Serena city.

disappears in the Atacama. ESO now plans to build a 42-metre European Extremely Large Telescope (E-ELT) 3,060 metres up in the Atacama, for observing stars 59 million light years away, in order to study red-shift galaxies that can tell us about the distant past of the universe.

The world's largest and most sensitive radio-telescope will be the Square Kilometre Array (SKA), which is currently being built in two desert locations in Southern Africa and Western Australia. When completed, the SKA will allow astronomers to glimpse the formation and evolution of the very first star formations and galaxies after the Big Bang, to explore the nature of gravity and perhaps to discover extra-terrestrial life.

Antarctica's cold, dry air makes it, too, an important station for optical astronomy. In contrast to the ferocious gales near the coast, the summits of the plateau have extremely stable air with minimal scintillation, as well as the darkest skies and the most transparent atmosphere of any Earth-based observing site. There are now observatories at the Amundsen-Scott South Pole Station where the 10-m South Pole Telescope is located, and Dome C, Dome A and Dome F are conducting optical, infrared and sub-millimetre astronomy to measure cosmic rays, gamma rays and neutrinos.[11]

European Southern Observatory, Paranal site. This aerial photograph of ESO's Very Large Telescope (VLT) demonstrates the superb quality of the observing site. In the foreground we see the domes of the four 8.2-m telescopes of the VLT and the control building, located at an altitude of 2,600 m on Cerro Paranal mountain, Chile. In the background is the snow-capped, 6,720-m-high volcano Llullaillaco, located 190 km further east on the Argentine border.

These scientific spin-offs from deserts may be crucial for the world's future needs. Generating power from a cheap and ever-renewable resource may bring nations closer to economic parity; locating ourselves within the universe may possibly provide a grander perspective that could make redundant the waste and devastation of wars.

Attractive as these potential benefits may be in a material sense, the insights that have emerged from cultural engagement with deserts may, in the long term, be even more important. Writers and film-makers have recreated from their experience or their imaginations the mystique, the challenge, the solitude and the silence to be encountered there, and their profound effect on the experiencing self. Since deserts defy the parameters of classical landscape art designed to simulate a nature under the domination of the observer, artists have discovered a renaissance in perception. There has also been a new awareness and appreciation

of indigenous desert cultures, their insights into the sacredness of the land and their relationship with it. The 'otherness' of deserts has come to epitomize a new perspective: the unexpected beauty of minimalism, the acknowledgement of, and respect for, dissenting values and a questioning of economic rationalism and materialism as pre-eminent goals for our planet.

Aerial view of the 10-m-diameter South Pole Telescope at the Amundsen-Scott South Pole Station.

THE WORLD'S MAJOR DESERTS

Name	Type	Area (sq. km)	Area (sq. miles)	Location
Antarctica	Polar	13,829,430	5,338159	Antarctica
Arabian	Subtropical	2,330,000	899,380	Saudi Arabia, Jordan, Iraq, Kuwait, Qatar, United Arab Emirates, Oman and Yemen
Atacama	Cool coastal	140,000	54,000	Chile and Peru
Chihuahuan	Subtropical	450,000	173,700	Mexico and United States
Gibson	Subtropical	155,000	59,830	Australia
Gobi	Cold Winter	1,300,000	501,800	Mongolia and China
Great Basin	Cold Winter	492,000	189,912	United States
Great Sandy	Subtropical	400,000	154,400	Australia
Great Victoria	Subtropical	647,000	249,742	Australia
Kalahari	Subtropical	900,000	347,400	Angola, Botswana, Namibia and South Africa

Karakum	Cold Winter	350,000	135,100	Turkmenistan
Kyzyl Kum	Cold Winter	300,000	115,800	Kazakhstan, Turkmenistan and Uzbekistan
Mojave	Subtropical	65,000	25,090	United States
Namib	Cool Coastal	81,000	31,266	Namibia and Angola
Patagonian	Cold Winter	670,000	258,620	Argentina and Chile
Sahara	Subtropical	9,100,000	3,512,600	Algeria, Chad, Djibouti, Egypt, Eritrea, Libya, Mali, Mauritania, Morocco, Niger, Sudan, Tunisia and Western Sahara
Simpson	Subtropical	145,000	55,970	Australia
Sonoran	Subtropical	310,000	119,660	Mexico and United States
Syrian	Subtropical	520,000	200,720	Syria, Jordan, Saudi Arabia and Iraq
Taklamakan	Cold Winter	270,000	104,220	China
Thar	Subtropical	200,000	77,200	India and Pakistan

GLOSSARY

alluvial fan: fan-shaped deposit formed where a fast-flowing stream flattens, slows and spreads, typically at the exit of a canyon on to a flatter plain

altiplano: the high tableland of central South America

Apsara: supernatural female spirits of the water or clouds, appearing in Hindu and Buddhist mythology and art

aquifer: layer of water-permeable underground rock that can store or transmit ground water

aurora australis: Southern Lights; the appearance of streamers or beams of coloured light in the sky near the South Magnetic Pole, caused by interaction of charged particles from the sun with atoms in the upper atmosphere

barchan: arc-shaped dune with two 'horns' that face downwind

Benguela current: broad northward-flowing ocean current in the eastern part of the South Atlantic Ocean

Bodhissatva: in Mahayana Buddhism, a being who devotes him/herself to seeking Buddhahood altruistically for the benefit of all

butte: narrow flat-topped hill of resistant rock with very steep sides; probably a former mesa

Cretaceous Period: a geologic time span from 145.5 MYA to 65.6 MYA. Following the Jurassic Period (199.6–145.5 MYA), it enjoyed a relatively warm climate, resulting in shallow inland seas

Desert Fathers (and Mothers): Christian hermits and monks (and nuns) who, following Anthony the Great, chose to live in the Egyptian desert around the third century CE

desertification: degradation of formerly fertile land to desert, usually resulting from deforestation, drought or inappropriate agricultural practices

desert pavement: thin surface layer of closely packed pebbles

diapause: delay in development in response to recurring adverse environmental conditions

Dreaming: (translation of the Aranda word *ulchurringa*, derived from *altjerri*, 'to dream'). In Australian Aboriginal culture the Dreaming is associated with the spirit world and specifically with the time when the Ancestral Spirits emerged from the Earth to create the features of the land, which remain imbued with their presence as sacred sites

dune: mound or ridge of sand formed by wind. They may be crescentic, star-shaped or linear (usually parallel ridges)

ephemeral: in botany, plants with a short life cycle, usually six to eight weeks

erg: sand 'sea' of shifting dunes

evapotranspiration: sum of water loss to the atmosphere through evaporation from bodies of water, soil, etc. and transpiration of water vapour through the stomata of plant leaves

fossil water: ground water that has been trapped in an aquifer for thousands, even millions of years, without being replenished from precipitation

gibber: pebbles covering large areas of Australian desert regions, notably Sturt Stony Desert; a type of desert pavement

Gondwana: the southern of the two ancient supercontinents (the other being Laurasia) formed between 550–500 MYA. About 184 MYA it began to break up, leaving Africa, India, South America, Australia and Antarctica as separate entities

halophilic: salt-loving

halophytic: salt-tolerant

hamada: (Arabic) hard, rocky plateau formed when wind removes fine sand particles, leaving gravel and boulders

Harmattan: the dry, dusty West African trade wind that blows south from the Sahara between the end of November and mid-March

Humboldt current: cold, low-salinity ocean current flowing northwest along the west coast of South America

hypolith: photosynthetic organism that lives under rocks in climatically extreme deserts such as Antarctica

ice blink: intense white glow at the horizon, resulting from the reflection of light off an ice field beyond

inselberg: isolated rock hill or small mountain arising abruptly from a plain

jinn: (Arabic) genies or supernatural spirits, often implying evil demons

Kaaba: (Arabic, 'The Cube'). Situated within the courtyard of the Al-Haram mosque in Mecca, it is the most sacred site of Islam. During the hajj pilgrims walk seven times counter-clockwise around it. According to the Qur'an Ibrahim (Abraham) and his son Ishmael built the Kaaba, in one corner of which was embedded the Black Stone brought to them by an angel.

katabatic wind: a down-slope, gravity-driven wind, blowing from mountains or plateaux

keffiyeh: (Arabic) traditional Arab man's head-covering; basically
a square cotton scarf of white or checked material, folded in half
to make a triangle and secured with a black rope circlet or *agal*

loma: (Spanish) small hill

mesa: (Spanish) broad, flat-topped hill rounded by cliffs and capped
with a resistant rock layer

mirage: optical phenomenon in which light rays are bent to produce
a transferred image of distant objects or the sky. In deserts this
frequently appears as a body of water, because the viewer desires this

Nabataeans: Arab people who built Petra some 2,000 years ago.
Originally nomadic, they became wealthy spice traders, gaining political
control over a wide area and adopting elements of Hellenistic culture

Orientalism: exotic trend in European art in the eighteenth and
nineteenth centuries involving depiction or imitation of Middle Eastern
cultures. Later the focus moved to the Far East, adopting elements of
Chinese and Japanese culture and art

pack ice: ice formed from frozen sea-water either at sea or locked to the
shore. It produces the expansion in area of Antarctica during the winter

pancake ice: rounded pieces of ice from a few centimetres to metres in
diameter and several centimetres thick with an elevated rim

paraselene: bright spot in the sky similar to a parhelion but formed
by refraction of moonlight

parhelion: optical effect of bright spots on the solar halo on either side
of the sun, formed by refraction of ice crystals in the atmosphere,
especially around sunset

phreatophyte: deep-rooted plant that obtains water from a permanent
ground supply or from the water table

plate tectonics: the theory that the earth's surface is divided into seven
or eight large tectonic plates that are continually moving. Earthquakes,
volcanic activity and mountain-building occur where the plates meet

playa: (Spanish) saline lake formed by evaporation

Puna: (Spanish) high, treeless plateau in the Peruvian Andes

quebrada: (Spanish) valley on the edge of the Atacama plateau with
a shallow stream flowing in it

reg: stony plain which may appear as cobbled pavements

salt pan: flat area, usually in desert regions, covered in salt and other
minerals

sastrugi: (Russian) wavelike ridges from centimetres to metres high
formed by wind on the surface of hard snow, parallel to the prevailing
wind direction

scintillation: 'twinkling' of stars caused by the Earth's atmosphere
diffracting starlight unevenly. It adversely affects astronomical observations

semi-arid: receiving between 25 and 50 cm of precipitation annually

stoma, pl. stomata: pore in the epidermis of leaves and stems through which exchanges of gases occurs

tagelmust: indigo-blue veil worn tightly wound around the face by Tuareg men

therianthrope: a human being changed into the shape of a non-human animal

Tuareg: nomadic pastoralists of North Africa speaking Berber-related languages

wadi: (Arabic) dry river bed that briefly supports vegetation after rain

xerophyte: a plant structurally adapted to survive in an area of limited water supply

REFERENCES

Preface

1 Ernest Giles, *Australia Twice Traversed: The Romance of Exploration*, 2 vols (London, 1889), vol. i, Book ii, p. 166.
2 Ibid., Book iii, p. 126.
3 Yi-Fu Tuan, 'Desert and Ice: Ambivalent Aesthetics in Landscape', in *Landscape, Natural Beauty and the Arts*, ed. Salim Kemal and Ivan Gaskell (Cambridge, 1993), pp. 146–7.

1 The Diversity of Deserts

1 P. J. Wyllie, *The Way the Earth Works: An Introduction to the New Global Geology and its Revolutionary Development* (New York, 1976), p. 211.
2 The thirteen countries the Sahara crosses are Western Sahara, Mauritania, Morocco, Algeria, Tunisia, Mali, Libya, Niger, Chad, Egypt, Sudan, Eritrea and Djibouti.
3 G. Grall, 'Cuatro Ciénegas: Mexico's Desert Aquarium', *National Geographic*, clxxxviii/4 (1995), pp. 84–97.
4 Joel Michaelsen, 'Colorado Desert Region Physical Geography', at www.geog.ucsb.edu, accessed 27 March 2013.
5 Donald Campbell set a land speed record of 648.73 km/h there in 1964.
6 Ernest Giles, *Australia Twice Traversed: The Romance of Exploration*, 2 vols (London, 1889), vol. ii, Book iv, p. 191.
7 Rebecca Courtney, 'Canning Stock Route: The Aboriginal Story', *Australian Geographic Online*, 15 December 2011, at www.australiangeographic.com.au.
8 C. T. Madigan, 'The Australian Sand-ridge Deserts', *Geographical Review*, xxvi/2 (1936), pp. 205–27; Mike Smith, 'Australian Deserts, Deserts Past: The Archaeology and Environmental

History of the Australian Deserts', Australian Bureau of Statistics
(2008), at www.abs.gov.au.

9 Australian Bureau of Statistics, *Year Book Australia* (Canberra,
2006), p. 13.

10 Paul C. Sereno, 'Dinosaur Death Trap: Gobi Desert Fossils Reveal
how Dinosaurs Lived', *Scientific American*, ccciv/3 (21 February
2011), at www.scientificamerican.com.

11 See Rio Tinto, 'Oyu Tolgoi' (2012), at www.riotinto.com.

12 Charles Darwin, *The Voyage of the Beagle* (Geneva, 1968), p. 455.

13 Boris Aleksandrovich Fedorovich and Agadjan G. Babaev,
'Karakum Desert', *Encyclopædia Britannica Online* (2011), at
www.britannica.com.

14 David B. Weishampel et al., 'Dinosaur Distribution', in
The Dinosauria, ed. David B. Weishampel, Peter Dodson and
Halszka Osmólska, 2nd edn (Berkeley, CA, 2004), pp. 517–606.

15 Mikhail Platonovich Petrov and Guy S. Alitto, 'The Takla Makan
Desert', *Encyclopædia Britannica Online* (2011), at
www.britannica.com.

16 Calogeo M. Santoto, Vivien G. Standen, Bernardo T. Arriaza and
Pablo A. Marquet, 'Hunter-gatherers on the Coast and Hinterland
of the Atacama Desert', in *23°s: Archaeology and Environmental
History of the Southern Deserts*, ed. Mike Smith and Paul Hesse
(Canberra, 2005), pp. 172–85.

17 Jonathan Amos, 'Chile Desert's Super-dry History', *BBC World
News* (8 December 2005), at www.bbc.co.uk/news.

18 V. Parro et al., 'A Microbial Oasis in the Hypersaline Atacama
Subsurface Discovered by a Life Detector Chip: Implications
for the Search for Life on Mars', *Astrobiology*, XI/10 (2011),
pp. 969–96.

19 M. D. Skogen, 'A Biophysical Model applied to the Benguela
Upwelling System', *South African Journal of Marine Science*, XXI
(1999), pp. 235–49; J. H. Van der Merwe, *National Atlas of South
West Afrika (Namibia)* (Windhoek, 1983).

20 Michael Mares, ed., *Deserts* (Norman, OK, 1999), p. 384.

21 E. M. Van Zinderen Bakker, 'Palynological Evidence for Late
Cenozoic Arid Conditions along the Namibian Coast from Holes
532 and 530 a, leg.75. Deep Sea Drilling Project', in *Initial Reports
of the Deep Sea Drilling Project*, ed. W. W. Hay, J. C. Sibuet et al.
(Washington, DC, 1984), vol. LIV, pp. 763–8.

22 Namibian Ministry of Mines and Energy, 'Geological Survey
of Namibia', n.d., at www.mme.gov.na, accessed 27 March 2013.

23 Areas of the lands surrounding the Arctic Ocean share some of the
desert characteristics of Antarctica but have not been discussed here
as they are relatively small – and shrinking with global warming.

24 Australian Government Antarctic Division, 'Antarctic Prehistory Facts' (2010), at www.antarctica.gov.au.

25 Ibid.

26 British Antarctic Survey, 'Volcanoes in Antarctica' (2007), at www.antarctica.ac.uk; British Antarctic Survey, 'Underwater Antarctic Volcanoes Discovered in the Southern Ocean' (2011), at www.antarctica.ac.uk.

27 Oxygen atoms give off red and green light; nitrogen molecules, blue and violet light.

28 Eric J. Steig et al., 'Warming of the Antarctic Ice-sheet Surface since 1957 International Geophysical Year', *Nature*, CCCCLVII/7228 (2009), pp. 459–62.

2 An Armoury of Adaptations

1 The Joshua tree was so named by nineteenth-century Mormon settlers who crossed the Mojave Desert. The tree's uplifted branches reminded them of the biblical story of Joshua reaching his hands up in prayer. Corey L. Gucker, *'Yucca brevifolia'*, in *Fire Effects Information System* (Fort Collins, CO, 2006), at www.fs.fed.us.

2 L. E. Gilbert, 'Ecological Consequences of Mesquite Fixation of Nitrogen', at http://uts.cc.utexas.edu, accessed 27 March 2013.

3 The ! of !nara represents the 'click' sound that is integral to the language of the !Kung people.

4 P. van Oosterzee, *The Centre: The Natural History of Australia's Desert Regions* (Chatswood, NSW, 1993), p. 74.

5 Bernard Eitel, 'Environmental History of the Namib Desert', in *23°S: Archaeology and Environmental History of the Southern Deserts*, ed. Mike Smith and Paul Hesse (Canberra, 2005), pp. 45–55.

6 W. Rauch, 'The Peruvian-Chilean Deserts', in *Hot Deserts and Shrublands*, ed. M. Evenari, I. Noy-Meir and D. W. Goodall (Amsterdam, 1985), p. 246.

7 Charles McCubbin, 'Desert Diary', *Aluminium*, X (December 1973), p. 6.

8 Van Oosterzee, *The Centre*, p. 80.

9 Mike Smith and Paul Hesse, 'Capricorn's Deserts', in *23°S*, ed. Smith and Hesse, p. 7.

10 Julia C. Jones and Benjamin P. Oldroyd, 'Nest Thermoregulation in Social Insects', *Advances in Insect Physiology*, XXIII (2007), pp. 153–92.

11 See University of Colorado at Boulder, 'Tiny Collectors: Harvester Ants' (2009), at http://cumuseum.colorado.edu.

12 A. R. Parker and C. R. Lawrence, 'Water Capture by a Desert Beetle', *Nature*, CDXIV/6859 (2001), pp. 33–4.

13 Thomas R. Van Devender, *Adaptations of Amphibians and Reptiles* (Tucson, AZ, 2011), at www.desertmuseum.org.
14 Van Oosterzee, *The Centre*, pp. 126–7.
15 Ibid., p. 127.
16 Ibid., pp. 112, 116.
17 Ibid., p. 115.
18 O. Oftedal, 'Nutritional Ecology of the Desert Tortoise in the Mojave and Sonoran Deserts', in *The Sonoran Desert Tortoise*, ed. T. R. Van Devender (Tucson, AZ, 2002), pp. 194–241.
19 Marc Tyler Nobleman, *Foxes* (New York, 2007), pp. 35–6.
20 The total world population of the Saharan cheetah is estimated at only 250 mature animals.
21 Daniel Thomas, 'Evolutionary Characteristic Allows Penguins to Adapt to Cold Climate', *Biology Letters* (2010), at http://rsbl.royalsocietypublishing.org.

3 Desert Cultures Past and Present

1 Peter Veth, 'Conclusion: Major Themes and Future Research Directions', in *Desert Peoples: Archaeological Perspectives*, ed. Peter Veth, Mike Smith and Peter Hiscock (Oxford, 2005), p. 299.
2 I. O. Rassooli, *History of the Arabs: The Arabian Peninsula* (2009), at www.islam-watch.org.
3 Gertrude Bell, *The Desert and the Sown* (London, 1985), p. 66.
4 Donald P. Cole, 'Where Have the Bedouin Gone?', *Anthropological Quarterly*, LXXVII/2 (2003), p. 257.
5 Bell, *The Desert and the Sown*, p. 67.
6 *Art and Life in Africa* (3 November 1998), at www.uiowa.edu.
7 Tamazight, spoken by 3–5 million people in Central Morocco, has over 300 related dialects. Ibid.
8 BBC World Service, 'Berbers: The Proud Raiders' (23 April 2001), at www.bbc.co.uk/worldserviceradio.
9 Peter Prengaman, 'Morocco's Berbers Battle to Keep from Losing Their Culture: Arab Minority Forces Majority to Abandon Native Language', *San Francisco Chronicle* (16 March 2001), at www.sfgate.com.
10 African Holocaust Society, 'People of Africa: Tuareg' (2004), at www.africanholocaust.net.
11 John Evans, 'Taoudenni Salt Mines' (1997), at www.johnevansphotography.net; N. Onishi, 'In Sahara Salt Mine, Life's not Too Grim', *New York Times* (13 February 2001), at www.nytimes.com.
12 Geraldine Brooks, *Nine Parts of Desire: The Hidden World of Islamic Women* (London, 1995), p. 22.

13 Human Rights Watch, 'Niger: Warring Sides Must End Abuses of Civilians' (2007), at www.hrw.org.

14 Human Rights Watch, 'Stemming the Flow: Other Abuses against Migrants and Refugees' (2006), at www.hrw.org.

15 As the terms 'San' and 'Bushmen' were originally derogatory appellations applied by others, '!Kung' (the name they call themselves) will be used here.

16 Anne I. Thackeray, 'Perspectives on Later Stone Age Hunter-gatherer Archaeology in Arid Southern Africa', in *Desert Peoples*, ed. Veth et al., p. 161; Bradshaw Foundation, 'The San Bushmen of the Drakensberg Mountains' (2011), at www.bradshawfoundation.com.

17 The Mongongo tree is *Ricinodendron rautanenii* Schinz. See Lee, *The !Kung San*, pp. 182–204.

18 Marshall Sahlins, *Stone Age Economics* (London, 1972), p. 9; Richard B. Lee, *The Dobe !Kung* (San Francisco, CA, 1979), p. 37.

19 Karim Sadr, 'Hunter-gatherers and Herders of the Kalahari during the Late Holocene', in *Desert Peoples*, ed. Veth et al., pp. 206, 210.

20 Ibid., pp. 216–17.

21 Survival International, 'African People and Culture: Bushmen/San', at www.africaguide.com, accessed 27 March 2013.

22 Richard Lee, *The Dobe Ju/'hoansi: Case Studies in Cultural Anthropology*, 3rd edn (Belmont, CA, 2003); Megan Biesele and Kxao Royal-/O/OO, 'The Ju/'hoansi of Botswana and Namibia', in *The Cambridge Encyclopedia of Hunters and Gatherers*, ed. Richard B. Lee and Richard Daly (Cambridge, 1999), pp. 205–9.

23 'Mungo Man' is the name given to one of two fossils discovered in 1974 near Lake Mungo in New South Wales. See M. Barbetti and H. Allen, 'Prehistoric Man at Lake Mungo, Australia, by 32000 years BP', *Nature*, CCXL/5375 (1972), pp. 46–8. The dating has been controversial, since different results have been given by the various methods, but the latest consensus is 40,000 years. J. M. Bowler et al., 'New Ages for Human Occupation and Climatic Change at Lake Mungo, Australia', *Nature*, CDXXI /6925 (2003), pp. 837–40

24 Douglas W. Bird and Rebecca Bliege Bird, 'Evolutionary and Ecological Understandings of the Economics of Desert Societies', in *Desert Peoples*, ed. Veth et al., pp. 87, 88; R. G. Kimber, '"Because It Is Our Country": The Pintupi and their Return to their Country, 1970–1990', in *23 °S: Archaeology and Environmental History of the Southern Deserts*, ed. Mike Smith and Paul Hesse (Canberra, 2005), pp. 349, 354.

25 Three hypothetical migration routes have been proposed: from the Amazon Basin over the high Andes; from northern Colombia via the Andes; and along the coast from Alaska. None has yet been definitively accepted.

26 Calogero M. Santoro et al., 'People of the Coastal Atacama Desert', in *Desert Peoples*, ed. Veth et al., pp. 250–52.
27 Ibid., pp. 248, 246.
28 Polyethylene mesh nets 4 m high and 10 m wide collect up to 5 litres of water per square metre, or 200 litres per day, from each net. See Michael Grimm, 'Water Solutions: Farming the Fog', Allianz Knowledge Site (4 March 2011), at http://knowledge.allianz.com.
29 Catherine S. Fowler, 'The Timbisha Shoshone of Death Valley', in *The Cambridge Encyclopedia of Hunters and Gatherers* (2006), at www.credoreference.com.
30 Boris Aleksandrovich Fedorovich and Agadjan G. Babaev, 'Karakum Desert', in *Encyclopaedia Britannica*, at www.britannica.com.
31 Angus M. Fraser, *The Gypsies*, 2nd edn (Oxford, 1995).
32 Colin Duly, *The Houses of Mankind* (London, 1979), pp. 86–7.
33 Nicholas Wade, 'A Host of Mummies, a Forest of Secrets', *New York Times* (15 March 2010), at www.nytimes.com.
34 Colin Thubron, 'The Secrets of the Mummies', *New York Review of Books* (May 12–25, 2011), pp. 17–18.
35 J. P. Mallory and Victor H. Mair, *The Tarim Mummies: Ancient China and the Mystery of the Earliest Peoples from the West* (London, 2000), p. 332.

4 Museums of Our Ancestors

1 Christopher Henshilwood, 'Prosjekt' (2002), at www.uib.no/personer.
2 Henri Lhote, *The Search for the Tassili Frescoes*, trans. Alan Houghton Brodrick (London, 1973).
3 J. David Lewis-Williams and T. A. Dowson, 'Through the Veil: San Rock Paintings and the Rock Face', *South African Archaeological Bulletin*, XLV (1990), pp. 5–16.
4 Per Michaelsen and Tasja W. Ebersole, 'The Bradshaw Rock Art System, NW Australia', *Adoranten* (2000), pp. 33–40.
5 Grahame L. Walsh, *Australia's Greatest Rock Art* (Bathurst, NSW, 1988), p. 222; Grahame L. Walsh, *Bradshaws: Ancient Rock Paintings of North-West Australia* (Geneva, 1994), p. 42.
6 Walsh, *Bradshaws*, p. 13.
7 Ibid., pp. 28–9.
8 Ibid., pp. 43–6.
9 Optically stimulated luminescence (OSL) and accelerator mass spectrometry (AMS) carbon dating of pollen grains recovered from a mud-wasp nest built over a Bradshaw painting indicate that the figures might be more than 17,000 years old. See Richard Roberts

et al., 'Luminescent Dating of Rock Art and Past Environments Using Mud-wasp Nests in Northern Australia', *Nature*, CCCLXXXVII (1997), pp. 696–9; Howard Morphy, *Aboriginal Art* (New York, 2004), p. 56.

10 Walsh, *Bradshaws*, p. 41.

11 Grahame L. Walsh, *Bradshaw Art of the Kimberley* (Toowong, Queensland, 2000), p. 444; Walsh, *Bradshaws*, pp. 58, 60.

12 J. D. Pettigrew, M. Nugent, A. McPhee and J. Wallman, 'An Unexpected, Stripe-faced Flying Fox in Ice Age Rock Art of Australia's Kimberley', *Antiquity*, LXXXII/318 (December 2008), www.antiquity.ac.uk.

13 Judith Ryan, *Images of Power: The Aboriginal Art of the Kimberley* (Melbourne, 1993), pp. 11–13.

14 Morphy, *Aboriginal Art*, pp. 55–6.

15 Robert Layton, 'Cultural Context of Hunter-gatherer Rock Art', *Man*, xx/3 (1985), p. 446.

16 In 1985 Warlpiri women produced diagrammatic picture maps as part of their evidence for the Mount Allen Land Claim. In 1997, 60 Kimberley men and women produced an 8-by-10-m canvas map indicating physical and spiritual sites as evidence for their title claim over a vast area of the Great Sandy Desert.

17 Bernardo T. Arriaza, Russell A. Hapke, and Vivien G. Standen, *Making the Dead Beautiful: Mummies as Art*, Archaeological Institute of America (1998), at www.archaeology.org.

18 Jinshi Fan, *The Caves of Dunhuang*, ed. and trans. Susan Whitfield (Hong Kong, 2010), pp. 7, 9.

19 M. Aurel Stein, *Ruins of Desert Cathay: Personal Narrative of Explorations in Central Asia and Western China*, 2 vols (London, 1912), (New York, 1912), vol. II, pp. 172, 176.

20 Aurel Stein, *On Ancient Central-Asian Tracks: Brief Narrative of Three Expeditions in Innermost Asia and Northwestern China* (Chicago, IL, 1964), p. xii.

21 Stein, *Ruins of Desert Cathay*, vol. I, pp. 473, 480, 487, 492.

22 Ibid., vol. II, p. 25.

23 Diamond Sutra, British Library, London. Ref. Or.8210/P.2, at www.bl.uk.

24 British Museum, 'Marc Aurel Stein', at www.britishmuseum.org, accessed 27 March 2013.

25 Fan, *The Caves of Dunhuang*, p. 249.

5 Desert Religions

1 The name 'Semitic' is derived from Shem the son of Noah. The Semitic tribes include the Hebrew, Arabic and Aramaic peoples.

2   See Barbara J. Sivertsen, *The Parting of the Sea: How Volcanoes, Earthquakes and Plagues Shaped the Story of the Exodus* (Princeton, NJ, 2009). The present-day Mt Sinai is not the Hebrew Bible one but what was then known as Mt Horeb.

3   T. E. Lawrence, *Seven Pillars of Wisdom* (Harmondsworth, 1962), chap. 3.

4   Zoroastrianism is the oldest known monotheistic religion, founded by the prophet Zoroaster in Iran 3,500 years ago, but it now has very few adherents.

5   W.O.E. Oesterley and T. H. Robinson, *Hebrew Religion: Its Origins and Development* (London, 1966), p. 155.

6   Gertrude Bell, *The Desert and the Sown* (London, 1985), p. 10.

7   See Matthew 9:14.

8   Yom Kippur, the Day of Atonement, is the only fast day prescribed in Mosaic law (Leviticus 14:27), though four others were later established to commemorate sad events of the Jewish people. See 'Feasting and Fast Days', www.jewishencyclopedia.com, accessed 27 March 2013.

9   Hershey H. Friedman, 'The Simple Life: The Case against Ostentation in Jewish Law', *Jewish Law* (July 2002), at www.jlaw.com.

10 Instructions on constructing the booths are found in Leviticus 23:29–43.

11 Robert Payne, *Jerome: The Hermit* (New York, 1951), p. 99.

12 John Chryssavgis, *In the Heart of the Desert: The Spirituality of the Desert Fathers and Mothers* (Bloomington, IN, 2008), p. 15.

13 Yi-Fu Tuan, 'Desert and Ice: Ambivalent Aesthetics', in *Landscape, Natural Beauty and the Arts*, ed. Salim Kemal and Ivan Gaskell (Cambridge, 1993), p. 144.

14 Rudolf Otto, *The Idea of the Holy* (Oxford, 1970), pp. 12–31.

15 R. B. Blakney, *Meister Eckhart: A Modern Translation* (New York, 1941), pp. 200–01.

16 These included evangelical revival movements in several Protestant churches leading to the formation of the Free Church of Scotland and the Plymouth Brethren, among others, the Oxford Movement in Britain and the Catholic revival in France.

17 By the 1860s there were Cook's package tours to the Middle East, via Alexandria and Egypt to Jerusalem and Damascus. See 'The Grand Tour: Map', www.iub.edu.

18 Medina had a strong Jewish enclave, while Christians and Zoroastrians had settlements on the southern coast of Arabia. Southern Arabia and Mecca absorbed a variety of religious ideas from abroad, including idolatry, animism, worship of the Kaaba and polytheism.

19 In Arabic the word *islam* means 'submission'.

20 Andrew B. Smith, 'Desert Solitude: The Evolution of Ideologies Among Pastoralists and Hunter-gatherers in Arid North Africa', in *Desert Peoples*, ed. Peter Veth, Mike Smith and Peter Hiscock (Oxford, 2005), p. 267.

21 C. Opler and M. E. Opler, *Apache Odyssey: A Journey Between Two Worlds* (New York, 1969), p. 24.

22 F. J. Gillen, 'Notes on some Manners and Customs of the Aborigines of the McDonnell Ranges belonging to the Arunta Tribe', in *Horn Scientific Expedition to Central Australia*, ed. B. Spencer (Melbourne and London, 1896), vol. IV.

23 See T.G.H. Strehlow, 'Personal Monototemism in a Polytotemic Community', in *Festschrift für Ad. E. Jensen*, ed. E. Haborland (Munich, 1964), pp. 723–53.

24 See Ronald M. Berndt, 'Territoriality and the Problem of Demarcating Socio-cultural Space', in *Tribes and Boundaries in Australia*, ed. Nicolas Peterson (Canberra, 1976), p. 137.

25 T.G.H. Strehlow, *Central Australian Religion*, Special Studies in Religions, vol. II (Bedford Park, South Australia, 1978), p. 16.

26 See Nancy Munn, 'Excluded Spaces: The Figure in the Australian Aboriginal Landscape', *Critical Inquiry*, XXII/3 (Spring 1996), pp. 446–65.

27 *Tjukurpa* is the Pitjanjatjara word; in Warlpirii it is *jukurrpa*.

28 See L. R. Hiatt and Rhys Jones, 'Aboriginal Conceptions of the Workings of Nature', in *Australian Science in the Making*, ed. R. W. Home (Cambridge, 1988), pp. 1–22.

29 Jack Davis, 'From the Plane Window', in *Black Life: Poems* (St Lucia, Queensland, 1992), p. 73.

30 Rex Ingamells, 'Uluru, An Apostrophe to Ayers Rock', in *The Jindyworobaks*, ed. Brian Elliott (St Lucia, Queensland, 1979), pp. 33–5.

31 David J. Tacey, *Edge of the Sacred* (Blackburn, Victoria, 1995), p. 8.

6 Travellers and Explorers

1 Ibn Battuta, *The Travels of Ibn Battuta, AD 1325–1354*, trans. C. Defremery and B. R. Sanguinetti (London, 2000), p. 51.

2 N. Levtzion and J.F.P. Hopkins, eds, *Corpus of Early Arabic Sources for West African History* (Cambridge, 1981), p. 132.

3 See Joseph J. Basile, 'When People Lived at Petra', *Archaeology Odyssey* (July–August 2000), pp. 14–25, 28–31, 59.

4 See Richard Burton, *A Personal Narrative of a Pilgrimage to Al-Medinah and Meccah* (London, 1855).

5 Charles M. Doughty, *Travels in Arabia Deserta* (London, 1926), p. 6.

6 'Some interest surrounds me for I am the first foreign woman who has ever been in these parts.' *The Letters of Gertrude Bell*, ed. Lady Florence Bell (London, 1927), p. 63.

7 Janet Wallach, *Desert Queen: The Extraordinary Life of Gertrude Bell* (London, 1996), p. 50.

8 Gertrude Bell, 'Preface', *The Desert and the Sown* (London, 1985), p. xx.

9 Sir Hugh Bell was a wealthy ironmaster and colliery owner. Sarah Graham-Brown, 'Introduction', Bell, *The Desert and the Sown*, p. v.

10 Bell's caravan required seven baggage animals, twelve horses, three muleteers, two servants and two soldiers as escort.

11 Sarah Graham-Brown, 'Introduction', *The Desert and the Sown*, p. ix.

12 Bell, *The Desert and the Sown*, pp. 1–2.

13 Diary entry to Doughty-Wylie, quoted in Wallach, *Desert Queen*, p. 118.

14 Freya Stark, *A Winter in Arabia* (London, 1940), pp. 246–7.

15 Edward Said, *Orientalism* (Harmondsworth, 1991), p. 224.

16 Wilfred Thesiger, *Arabian Sands* (Harmondsworth, 1964), pp. 37–8.

17 Ibid., p. 18.

18 Jeannette Mirsky, 'Introduction' to Aurel Stein, *On Ancient Central-Asian Tracks* (Chicago, IL, 1964), p. 2.

19 Ella K. Maillart, *Turkestan Solo: One Woman's Journey from the Tien Shin to the Kizil Kum* (London, 1938), p. 33.

20 Ibid., p. 324.

21 Ibid., p. 133.

22 Mildred Cable with Francesca French, *The Gobi Desert* (London, 1950), p. 172.

23 Ibid., p. 276.

24 Ibid., p. 23.

25 Ibid., pp. 289–93.

26 Ibid., pp. 63–4.

27 Ibid., p. 287.

28 Ibid., p. 172.

29 Charles Blackmore, *Crossing the Desert of Death: Through the Fearsome Taklamakan* (London, 1995), p. 7.

30 Ibid., p. 166.

31 Ernest Giles, *Australia Twice Traversed*, 2 vols (London, 1889), vol. II, Book III, p. 202.

32 Charles Sturt, *Narrative of an Expedition into Central Australia, 1844–45* (London, 1849), vol. I, p. 265.

33 Charles Sturt, *Journal of the Central Australian Expedition, 1844–5*, ed. J. Waterhouse (London, 1984), p. 45.

34 See the dynamic painting of this scene by Nicholas Chevalier, *Memorandum of the Start of the Exploring Expedition*, 1860, oil on canvas, held in the Art Gallery of South Australia, Adelaide.

35 J. S. Keltie and H. R. Mill, eds, *Report of the Sixth International Geographical Congress, Held in London, 1895* (London, 1896), p. 780.

36 Ernest Shackleton, *The Heart of the Antarctic*, 2 vols (New York, 1999), vol. I, p. I.

37 Roald Amundsen, *The South Pole*, trans. A. G. Chater, 2 vols (London, 1912), vol. I, pp. xxix–xxx.

38 Edward J. Larson, *Empire of Ice: Scott, Shackleton, and the Heroic Age of Antarctic Science* (New Haven, CT, 2011), pp. 145, 148.

39 Ursula K. Le Guin, 'Heroes', in *Dancing at the End of the World* (New York, 1989), p. 175.

40 Mawson declined Scott's invitation to participate in his *Terra Nova* expedition, seeing it as a mere race to the Pole.

41 Lennard Bickel, *Mawson's Will: The Greatest Polar Survival Story Ever Written* (Hanover, NH, 2000).

42 Byrd's team had 31 receivers, 24 transmitters and five radio engineers.

43 Richard E. Byrd, *Alone* (New York, 1995), p. 4.

44 Ibid., p. 161.

45 Charles Laseron, *Diary*, 23 November 1912. Mitchell Library, State Library of New South Wales, Sydney, ML MSS385.

46 For navigators in polar seas, ice blink indicates there is nothing but ice ahead.

47 Charles Harrisson, *Diary*, 2 October 1912, Mitchell Library, State Library of New South Wales, Sydney, ML MSS386.

48 Unlike Mawson, Jarvis had a film crew following him, doctors checking his health and other safety precautions, but essentially he did what Mawson had done. See *Mawson: Life and Death in Antarctica* (Orana Films, 2007) and *Mawson: Life and Death in Antarctica* (Melbourne, 2008).

49 See Penelope Debelle, 'Elation for Adelaide Adventurer Tim Jarvis as Epic Antarctic Trek Ends', www.adelaidenow.com.au, 11 February 2013.

50 Greg Callaghan, '10 Questions with Tim Jarvis, Adventurer and Environmental Scientist, 46', *Weekend Australian Magazine* (29–30 September 2012), p. 8.

7 Deserts of the Imagination

1 The statue reached London in 1818 shortly after the publication of Shelley's poem.

2 Percy Bysshe Shelley, 'Ozymandias' [1818], in *Shelley: A Selection*, ed. Isabel Quigly (Harmondsworth, 1956), p. 107.

3   See Bernard Smith, 'Coleridge's *Ancient Mariner* and Cook's Second Voyage', in *Imagining the Pacific: In the Wake of the Cook Voyages* (Melbourne, 1992), chap. 6, pp. 135–71.

4   John Livingston Lowes, *The Road to Xanadu: A Study in the Ways of the Imagination* (London, 1955), pp. 103–311.

5   Samuel Taylor Coleridge, 'The Rime of the Ancient Mariner', in *The Complete Poems*, ed. William Keach (London, 1997), p. 169.

6   James Elroy Flecker, 'The Gates of Damascus', in *The Collected Poems*, p. 151.

7   H. Rider Haggard, quoted in Patrick Brantlinger, *Rule of Darkness: British Literature and Imperialism, 1830–1914* (Ithaca, NY, 1988), p. 239.

8   P. C. Wren, *Beau Geste* (Ware, Herts, 1994), p. 1.

9   J.-M.G. Le Clézio, *Desert*, trans. C. Dickson (London, 2010), pp. 1–2.

10 Antoine de Saint-Exupéry, *Wind, Sand and Stars* (Harmondsworth, 1973), pp. 63, 75.

11 Laura Marks, 'Asphalt Nomadism: The New Desert in Arab Independent Cinemas', in *Landscape and Film*, ed. Martin Lefebre (London, 2006), pp. 1–30.

12 John C. Van Dyke, *The Desert* (New York, 1901), pp. 26, 56.

13 For example, Alexander Ernest Favenc, *The Secret of the Australian Desert* (1896); George Scott, *The Last Lemurian* (1898); Alexander McDonald, *The Lost Explorers* (1906).

14 See, for example, James F. Hogan, *The Lost Explorer* (1890), and Ernest Favenc, *The Secret of the Australian Desert* (1896).

15 See Roslynn D. Haynes, *Seeking the Centre: The Australian Desert in Literature, Art and Film* (Cambridge, 1998), pp. 129–42.

16 C.E.W. Bean, *The Dreadnought of the Darling* (London, 1911), pp. 317–18.

17 Pene Greet and Gina Price, *Frost Bytes* (Sydney, 1995); Robin Burns, *Just Tell Them I Survived!: Women in Antarctica* (Sydney, 2001).

18 Ursula K. Le Guin, 'Sur', in *The Penguin Book of Modern Fantasy by Women*, ed. Susan Williams and Richard Glyn Jones (London, 1995), pp. 389–90.

19 Barcroft Boake, 'Where the Dead Men Lie', in *The Penguin Book of Australian Ballads*, ed. Philip Butterss and Elizabeth Webby (Ringwood, Victoria, 1993), pp. 242–3.

20 A British tourist, Peter Falconio, travelling from Alice Springs towards Darwin with his girlfriend, was stopped by a man pretending to warn him of a problem with his vehicle. Falconio was shot by the stranger, who then kidnapped the woman and drove off. The woman escaped but Falconio's body has not been found. See 'Murdoch v The Queen [2007] NTCCA 1', 10 January 2007, www.supremecourt.nt.gov.au.

21 Poe uses the word 'Simoon' figuratively and for effect since it refers specifically to a sand-laden wind blowing in the Sahara, the Middle East and the Arabian deserts.

22 The film of 1951 is set in the Arctic, perhaps as a reference to the Cold War at that time. The films of 1982 and 2011, like Campbell's story, are set in Antarctica.

23 Pierre Loti was the nom de plume of Julien Marie Viaud (1850– 1923).

24 Pierre Loti, *The Desert*, trans. Jay Paul Minn (Salt Lake City, UT, 1993), pp. 14–15.

25 E.L. Grant Watson, *Daimon* (London, 1925), p. 315.

26 Randolph Stow, *Tourmaline* (Sydney, 1963), p. 7.

27 Randolph Stow, Poem 1 of 'From the Testament of Tourmaline', in *A Counterfeit Silence: Selected Poems* (Sydney, 1969), pp. 71–5.

28 Stow, *Tourmaline*, pp. 220–21.

29 Patrick White, 'The Prodigal Son', in *Australian Letters*, ed. Geoffrey Dutton and Max Harris, 1/3 (1958), p. 8.

30 Patrick White, *Voss* (Harmondsworth, 1963), pp. 87–8.

31 Patrick White, Letter to Ben Huebsch, 11 September 1956, in *Patrick White, Letters*, ed. David Marr (Sydney, 1994), p. 108.

32 Yi-Fu Tuan, 'Desert and Ice: Ambivalent Aesthetics in Landscape', in *Landscape, Natural Beauty and the Arts*, ed. Salim Kemal and Ivan Gaskell (Cambridge, 1993), p. 155.

33 White, *Voss*, p. 446.

8 Deserts in Western Art

1 The goat died of exhaustion after twelve days and, unable to find another, Hunt completed the painting in England.

2 Edward Lear, quoted in Gérard-Georges Lemaires, *The Orient in Western Art* (Paris, 2001), p. 174.

3 George Lambert's *The Road to Jericho* (1919) influenced Hans Heysen.

4 *Boston Evening Transcript* (5 December 1855), p. 1, quoted in *New Worlds from Old: 19th Century Australian and American Landscapes*, ed. Elizabeth Johns, Andrew Sayers and Elizabeth Mankin Kornhauser with Amy Ellis (Canberra, 1998), p. 117.

5 Quoted in Lisa Messenger, 'Georgia O'Keeffe', *Metropolitan Museum of Art Bulletin*, XLII/2 (1984), p. 43.

6 Quoted in Lisa Mintz Messenger, *Georgia O'Keeffe* (New York, 1988), p. 72.

7 Georgia O'Keeffe, *Black Mesa Landscape, New Mexico/Out Back of Marie's II*, 1930, oil on canvas, Georgia O'Keeffe Museum, Santa Fe.

8 Edward Frome, *First View of the Salt Desert – Called Lake Torrens*, 1843, watercolour on paper, Art Gallery of South Australia, Adelaide.

9 Hans Heysen, Letter to Lionel Lindsay, quoted in Colin Thiele, *Heysen of Hahndorf* (Adelaide, 1968), p. 202.

10 Hans Heysen, Letter to Sydney Ure Smith, 1926, quoted in *Hans Heysen Centenary Retrospective, 1877–1977* (Adelaide, 1977).

11 Hans Heysen, *Guardian of the Brachina Gorge*, 1937, watercolour over charcoal, National Gallery of Victoria, Melbourne.

12 Hans Heysen, Letter to Lionel Lindsay, 23 August 1928, quoted in Thiele, *Heysen of Hahndorf*, p. 205.

13 Russell Drysdale, *The Walls of China (Gol Gol)*, 1945, oil on hardboard, Art Gallery of New South Wales, Sydney.

14 Russell Drysdale, *Man Feeding His Dogs*, 1941, oil on canvas, Queensland Art Gallery, Brisbane.

15 Cynthia Nolan, *Outback* (London, 1962), p. 31.

16 Quoted in Sandra McGrath and John Olsen, *The Artist and the Desert* (Sydney, 1981), p. 60.

17 Sidney Nolan, in Elwyn Lynn and Sidney Nolan, *Sidney Nolan: Australia* (Sydney, 1979), p. 13.

18 See Roslynn D. Haynes, *Seeking the Centre: The Australian Desert in Literature, Art and Film* (Cambridge, 1998), pp. 212–15.

19 Barrett Reid, 'A Landscape of a Painter: The Sidney Nolan Retrospective Exhibition', *Art and Australia*, xxv/2 (1987), p. 181

20 Stephen J. Pyne, *The Ice: A Journey to Antarctica* (Iowa City, 10, 1986), pp. 151, 152.

21 This image appeared as an engraving (Volume 1, Plate 30) in James Cook, *A Voyage Towards the South Pole and Round the World* (London, 1777).

22 Louis Bernacchi (1876–1942) was a member of Carsten Borchgrevink's Southern Cross expedition (1898–1900) and then of Scott's Discovery expedition (1901–04). Trained in astronomy and physics, he was awarded the Royal Geographical Society Medal, the King's Antarctic Medal and the Légion d'honneur.

23 G. E. Fogg and David Smith, *The Explorations of Antarctica: The Last Unspoiled Continent* (London, 1990), p.78.

24 Lynne Andrews, personal communication, 21 June 2012.

25 Les Murray, 'Equanimity', in *Collected Poems* (Melbourne, 1994), p. 180.

9 Exploitation and Opportunity

1 United Nations Environment Programme, 'Status of the World's Deserts', in *Global Deserts Outlook* (2006), at www.unep.org.

2 The Global Assessment of Human-Induced Soil Degradation (GLASOD), based on UN expert opinion (UNEP 1997).

3 'Desert Life Threatened by Climate Change and Human Exploitation', *Independent*, 5 June 2006, at www.independent.co.uk.

4 Uzbekistan withdraws 14,000 cubic metres of water per hectare per day from the Amu Darya. Over 1.47 million hectares this amounts to over 20 cubic km of water annually. Environmental Justice Foundation, at www.ejfoundation.org.

5 'South Aral Sea "Gone in 15 Years"', *New Scientist*, 21 July 2003, at www.newscientist.com.

6 'Turkmenistan's "Door to Hell"', 25 March 2006, at www.gadling.com.

7 Hugo I. Romero, Pamela Smith and Alexis Vásquez, 'Global Changes and Economic Globalization in the Andes: Challenges for Developing Nations', in *Alpine Space – Man and Environment*, vol. VII (Innsbruck, 2009).

8 'CNIC Naval Air Weapons Station China Lake', at http://www.cnic.navy.mil/chinalake.

9 John Cooper, 'Biosecurity and Quarantine Guidelines for ACAP Breeding Sites', August 2011, at www.acap.aq.

10 See 'Plugging the World into Desert Sun', *Sydney Morning Herald* (23 February 2011), at ww.smh.com.au.

11 Michael G. Burton, 'Astronomy in Antarctica', *Astronomy and Astrophysics Review*, XVIII/4 (2010), pp. 417–69.

SELECT BIBLIOGRAPHY

Andrews, Lynne, *Antarctic Eye: The Visual Journey* (Mt Rumney, Tasmania, 2007)

Armstrong, Karen, *Islam: A Short History* (New York, 2000)

Bell, Gertrude, *The Desert and the Sown* (London, 1985)

Bickell, Lennard, *Mawson's Will: The Greatest Polar Survival Story Ever Written* (Hanover, NH, 2000)

Blackmore, Charles, *Crossing the Desert of Death: Through the Fearsome Taklamakan* (London, 1995)

Byrd, Richard E., *Alone* (New York, Tokyo and London, 1995)

Cable, Mildred, with Francesca French, *The Gobi Desert* (London, 1950)

Cherry-Garrard, Apsley, *The Worst Journey in the World* (London, 1994)

Coleridge, Samuel Taylor, 'The Rime of the Ancient Mariner', in *The Complete Poems*, ed. William Keach (London, 1997), pp. 166–80

Costello, D. F., *The Desert World* (New York, 1972)

Davidson, Robyn, *Tracks* (London, 1980)

Fan, Jinshi, *The Caves of Dunhuang*, ed. and trans. Susan Whitfield (Hong Kong, 2010)

Haynes, Roslynn D., *Seeking the Centre: The Australian Desert in Literature, Art and Film* (Cambridge, New York and Melbourne, 1998)

Huntford, Roland, *The Last Place on Earth* (London, 1985)

Keneally, Thomas, *A Victim of the Aurora* (London, 1977)

Larson, Edward J., *Empire of Ice: Scott, Shackleton, and the Heroic Age of Antarctic Science* (New Haven, CT, 2011)

Lawrence, T. E., *The Seven Pillars of Wisdom: A Triumph* (Harmondsworth, 1962)

Le Clézio, J.-M.G., *Desert*, trans. C. Dickson (London, 2010)

LeGuin, Ursula, 'Sur', in *The Penguin Book of Modern Fantasy by Women*, ed. Susan Williams and Richard Glyn Jones (London, 1995), pp. 389–90

Lee, Richard B., *The !Kung San: Men, Women, and Work in a Foraging Society* (Cambridge, 1979)

Lemaires, Gérard-Georges, *The Orient in Western Art* (Paris, 2000)

Lewis-Williams, J. D., *The Rock Art of Southern Africa* (Cambridge, 1983)

Lhote, Henri, *The Search for the Tassili Frescoes: The Story of Prehistoric Rock-Paintings of the Sahara*, trans., Alan Houghton Brodrick (London, 1973)

Maillart, Ella K., *Turkestan Solo: One Woman's Expedition from the Tien Shan to the Kizil Kum*, trans. John Rodker (London, 1938)

Mallory, J. P., and Victor H. Mair, *The Tarim Mummies: Ancient China and the Earliest Peoples from the West* (London, 2000)

Marks, Laura, 'Asphalt Nomadism: The New Desert in Arab Independent Cinemas', in *Landscape and Film*, ed. Martin Lefebvre (London, 2006), pp. 1–30

Mawson, Douglas, *The Home of the Blizzard: The Story of the Australasian Antarctic Expedition, 1911–1914* (London, 1915)

Messenger, Lisa Mintz, *Georgia O'Keeffe* (New York, 1988)

Morphy, Howard, *Aboriginal Art* (New York, 2004)

Oesterley, W.O.E., and Theodore H. Robinson, *Hebrew Religion: Its Origin and Development* (London, 1949)

Oosterzee, Penny van, *The Centre: The Natural History of Australia's Desert Regions* (Chatswood, NSW, 1993)

Otto, Rudolf, *The Idea of the Holy*, trans. John W. Harvey (London, 1958)

Panter-Brick, Catherine, Robert H. Layton and Peter Rowley-Conwy, eds, *Hunter-Gatherers: An Interdisciplinary Perspective* (Cambridge, 2001)

Pyne, Stephen J., *The Ice: A Journey to Antarctica* (Iowa City, 1986)

Ryan, Judith, *Images of Power: The Aboriginal Art of the Kimberley* (Melbourne, 1993)

Sahlins, Marshall, *Stone Age Economics* (London, 1972)

Saint-Exupéry, Antoine de, *Wind, Sand and Stars* (Harmondsworth, 1973)

Said, Edward W., *Orientalism: Western Conceptions of the Orient* (Harmondsworth, 1991)

Smith, Mike, and Paul Hesse, eds, *23°S: Archaeology and Environmental History of the Southern Deserts* (Canberra, 2005)

Stark, Freya, *A Winter in Arabia* (London, 1940)

——, *The Valleys of the Assassins and other Persian Travels* (London, 1940)

Stein, M. Aurel, *On Ancient Central-Asian Tracks: Brief Narrative of Three Expeditions in Innermost Asia and Northwestern China* (Chicago, IL, 1964)

——, *Ruins of Desert Cathay: Personal Narrative of Explorations in Central Asia and Western China*, 2 vols (London, 1912)

Stewart, Douglas, *Fire on the Snow* (Sydney, 1963)

Stow, Randolph, *Tourmaline* (Sydney, 1963)

Thesiger, Wilfred, *Arabian Sands* (Harmondsworth, 1964)

Tuan, Yi-Fu, 'Desert and Ice: Ambivalent Aesthetics', in *Landscape, Natural Beauty and the Arts*, ed. Salim Kemal and Ivan Gaskell (Cambridge, 1993), pp. 139–57

Van der Post, Laurens, *The Lost World of the Kalahari* (Harmondsworth, 1972)

Veth, Peter, Mike Smith and Peter Hiscock, *Desert Peoples: Archaeological Perspectives* (Oxford, 2003)

Wallach, Janet, *Desert Queen: The Extraordinary Life of Gertrude Bell* (London, 1996)

Walsh, Grahame L., *Australia's Greatest Rock Art* (Bathurst, NSW, 1988)

——, *Bradshaws: Ancient Rock Paintings of North-West Australia* (Geneva, 1994)

——, *Bradshaw Art of the Kimberley* (Toowong, Qld, 2000)

Watson, E. L. Grant, *Daimon* (London, 1925)

White, Patrick, *Voss* (Harmondsworth, 1963)

ASSOCIATIONS AND WEBSITES

Art Gallery of New South Wales
www.artgallery.nsw.gov.au

Australian Antarctic Division
www.antarctica.gov.au

BBC Religions
www.bbc.co.uk/religion/religions

Bradshaw Foundation
www.bradshawfoundation.com

British Antarctic Survey
www.antarctica.ac.uk

Desert Research Institute
www.dri.edu

European Space Agency
www.esa.int

Georgia O'Keeffe Museum
www.okeeffemusuem.org

Indigenous Peoples of Africa Coordinating Committee (IPACC)
www.ipacc.org.za

International Dun Huang Project: The Silk Road Online
http://idp.bl.uk

Journal of Cultural Geography
www.tandfonline.com

NASA (National Aeronautics and Space Administration)
www.nasa.gov

Scientific Committee on Antarctic Research
www.astronomy.scar.org

Scott Polar Research Institute, University of Cambridge
www.spri.cam.ac.uk

Society for Range Management
www.rangelands.org

Square Kilometre Array Telescope
www.skatelescope.org

The Silk Road Foundation
www.silkroadfoundation.org

United Nations Convention to Combat Desertification
www.unccd.int

United Nations Environment Programme, Global Deserts Outlook
www.unep.org/geo/gdoutlook

University of California Museum of Paleontology
www.ucmp.berkeley.edu/glossary/gloss5/biome/deserts

ACKNOWLEDGEMENTS

I am indebted to Daniel Allen, and Michael Leaman of Reaktion Books, for the invitation to write this book. It has been a most stimulating and rewarding experience. The encouragement of my family and friends has been an important factor in sustaining my enthusiasm during the long period of research and writing, and I thank them most sincerely.

I am also indebted to the following for permissions to quote from original or copyright material: Lynn Andrews and Christian Clare Robinson for allowing me to reproduce their wonderful paintings; Elizabeth Hawes for allowing me to reproduce the works of her late husband, David Smith; Les Murray for permission to quote from 'Equanimity', in *Collected Poems* (Melbourne, 1994), p. 180; and OMF (Overseas Missionary Fellowship) International for permission to use the archived photograph of Evangeline and Francesca French and Mildred Cable. Jack Davis, 'From the Plane Window', in *Black Life: Poems* (St Lucia, Queensland, 1992), p. 73, reproduced by arrangement with the Licensor, The Jack Davis Estate, c/- Curtis Brown (Aust) Pty Ltd.

PHOTO ACKNOWLEDGEMENTS

The author and publishers wish to express their thanks to the below sources of illustrative material and/or permission to reproduce it. Locations of some artworks are also given below.

Photos Peter and Christine Alexander: pp. 43, 47, 54; photo ALMA (ESO/ NAOJ/NRAO)/L. Calçada (ESO): p. 204; collection the artist (Lynne Andrews): p. 195 (top); courtesy Atlas Obscura: p. 25; photo Dr Jamila Bargach: p. 79; Bibliothèque Nationale, Paris: p. 120; photo Brian Boyle (CSIRO): p. 203; courtesy Bradshaw Foundation: pp. 93, 94, 95; British Library, London: p. 105; courtesy Brooklyn Museum, New York: p. 182; photo courtesy Robin Burns: p. 139; photo Captmondo: p. 26; Carly Googles Blogspot .com: pp. 148–9; from Samuel Taylor Coleridge, *The Rime of the Ancient Mariner* (London, 1876): p. 150; Cologne University Botanical Collection: p. 42; from James Cook, *A voyage towards the South Pole, and round the World. Performed in His Majesty's ships the Resolution and Adventure, in the years 1772, 1773, 1774, and 1775. Written by James Cook, Commander of the Resolution . . . In two volumes illustrated with maps and charts . . .* (London, 1777): p. 188; photo de Benutzer: Kookaburra: p. 168; courtesy Françoise Dussart: p. 98; Fondazione Contini Bonacossi, Florence: p. 117 (left); photo Glenn Grant, National Science Foundation: p. 208; photo Gruban, courtesy Getintravel .com: p. 92; courtesy Elizabeth Hawes: p. 193; Hearst Castle, San Simeon, California: p. 174 (foot); photo H. H. Heyer (ESO): p. 205; photo G. Hüde- pohl (ESO) (atacamaphoto.com): p. 206; photo Al-Jazeera: p. 121; courtesy R. G. Kimber: p. 97; Lady Lever Art Gallery, Port Sunlight: p. 179; photos Library of Congress, Washington, DC: pp. 80, 85, 174 (top); photo Daniel Luong-van: p. 36; photo Joe Mastroianni (National Science Foundation): p. 35; from the *Maqāmāt al-Harīrī* of Abū Muhammad al-Qāsim ibn Ali ibn Muhammad ibn Uthman al-Harīrī, illustrated by Yahyā ibn Mahmūd al-Wāsitī: p. 120; photo Baptiste Marcel: p. 131; photo Mhwater: p. 75; Minneapolis Institute of Arts, Minneapolis, Minnesota: p. 177; Museum of Fine Arts, Boston: pp. 109, 178; photos NASA/GSFC/METI/ERSDAC/JAROS, and U.S./Japan ASTER Science Team: pp. 16, 27; Collection National Maritime Museum, Greenwich: p. 190; published with permission from OMF (Overseas Missionary Fellowship) International www. omf.org: p. 136; photo K. Otpushcheia: p. 179; Paleozoological Museum of China: p. 26; photo Nick Powell (National Science Foundation): p. 34; photos Sergei Mikhailovich Prokudin-Gorskii: pp. 80, 85; photo Qfl247: pp. 28–9; photo Rabanus Flavus: p. 117 (right); photo Jeremy Richards/ Shutterstock.com: p. 82; collection the artist (Christian Clare Robertson): pp. 194, 195 (foot); photo Roke: p. 142; photo Alexander Romanovich/ Shutterstock.com: p. 86; The Rosewood Corporation, Dallas, Texas: p. 180; courtesy State Library of Victoria: p. 184; from M. Aurel Stein, *From Ruins of Desert Cathay: Personal Narrative of Explorations in Central Asia and Westernmost China*, vol. I (London, 1912): p. 102; vol. II (London, 1912): pp. 106, 134; photo Sullynyflhi: p. 41; photo Tentoila at en.wikipedia: p. 116; photo Jarek Tuszynski: p. 44; photo U.S. Navy, National Science Foundation: p. 147; photo Vanilla Travel: p. 23; photo Cresalde Jumbas Victoriano: p. 67 (foot); photos Wang Da-Gang (courtesy *New York Times*, 15 March 2010): p. 87; photo Mark A. Wilson: p. 20.

Ian Duffy, the copyright holder of the image on p. 62, **magharebia**, the copyright holder of the image on p. 14 (foot), **Umberto Salvagnin**, the copyright holder of the image on p. 57, **Tanenhaus**, the copyright holder of the image on p. 68, **Pablo Trincado**, the copyright holder of the image on p. 101, and **Faraz Usmani**, the copyright holder of the image on p. 84, have published these online under conditions imposed by a Creative Commons Attribution 2.0 Generic license; **Boston at en.wikipedia**, the copyright holder of the image on p. 90, **Ed Brambley**, the copyright holder of the image on p. 67 (top), **flydime**, the copyright holder of the image on p. 201, **Andries Oudshoorn**, the copyright holder of the image on pp. 18–19, **Rosino**, the copyright holder of the image on p. 9, and **Whinging Pom**, the copyright holder of the image on p. 99, have published these online under conditions imposed by a Creative Commons Attribution-Share Alike 2.0 Generic license; **Luca Galuzzi**, the copyright holder of the images on pp. 12, 14 (top), 31 and 91, and **Dustin Ramsey (Kralizec)**, the copyright holder of the image on p. 100, have published these online under conditions imposed by a Creative Commons Attribution-Share Alike 2.5 Generic license; **Sigismund von Dobschütz**, the copyright holder of the image on p. 138, **DVL2**, the copyright holder of the image on p. 72, **Dysmorodrepanis**, the copyright holder of the image on p. 42, **FlyingToaster**, the copyright holder of the image on p. 53, **Grauesel**, the copyright holder of the image on p. 113, **H. Grobe**, the copyright holder of the image on p. 71, **Jörn Heise**, the

INDEX